Extreme Environment Embedded Systems

Patrick H. Stakem

17th in the Computer Architecture Series

2nd edition

(c) 2015, 2017

Introduction..4
   Author..4
What is an Embedded system?...5
   Embedded processors...7
   Security..7
   Reliability..9
   Power Concerns, and the Cost of Computation........................10
   Standards...11
   Mobile platforms..14
   Flight Platforms..14
   Advanced battery and motor technology.................................14
   Open Source versus Proprietary...15
   An Architectural Model...17
      NASREM..17
      Real Time Control System (RCS).................................19
   Security..21
   Testing...22
   Self-monitoring and cross monitoring.....................................23
Harsh and Extreme Environments...24
Domains..27
   Ground...27
   Underground..27
   Desert..28
   Air..29
   Water/underwater..30
   Nuclear Plants...31
   Inside the human body...33
   Inside the car...34
   Space 36
      Radiation Effects...36
      Thermal issues..43
      Mechanical issues...43
      ESD sensitivity..44
      Bad Parts...44
   Underwater..45
   In the volcano..46
   Polar Regions..47

Examples of Embedded Systems in Extreme Environments........49
   Automotive Electronics...49
   Down the borehole...49
   NASA Rovers in Antarctica......................................50
   Greenland Rover (Grover) 51
   Lorax – Life on Ice...54
   Nereid-under-Ice..55
   Exploring our Solar System.....................................55
     Exploring the Moon...55
     Exploring the Sun...57
     Exploring Mercury..58
     Exploring Venus...59
     Exploring the Asteroids.....................................60
     Exploring Comets..60
     Exploring Mars..61
     Exploring the Gas Giants....................................69
     Exploring Pluto, and beyond.................................72
Case studys, system failures in Harsh environments....................73
   Aerospace..73
   Launch Vehicle Reliability.......................................73
   Titan Launch Vehicle..73
   Ariane 5...74
   Others...76
   Soyuz TMA-1 flight computer problem.............................76
   Phobos-Grunt...77
Transportation..80
   Air France 447, and the Automation Paradox.......................80
   X-15, pushing the limits...82
Wrap-up...83
Glossary 84
References..87
Resource..91
If you enjoyed this book, you might also be interested in some of
these...92

Introduction

This book covers the topic of embedded systems in Extreme Environments. The obvious extreme is outer space beyond our planet. However, these are many terrestrial harsh environments with parameters beyond room temperature and pressure. First and foremost, the embedded system must function properly. But we also have to consider the environment it is working in. We're not covering embedded systems sitting on the bench here. Even under the hood of a car, the environment is threatening to the many controllers needed for the car's operation.

Generally, if you're uncomfortable, your embedded electronics is uncomfortable. We will discuss embedded systems at the top level, and look at the classes of extreme environments, both on Earth and elsewhere in our solar system. Then we can look at some of the adjustments that have to be made in the embedded systems to operate in these environments, and the monitoring required to make sure they are still operating correctly

Author

The author received his BSEE from Carnegie Mellon University, and Masters in Computer Science and Applied Physics from the Johns Hopkins University. He has worked in the aerospace sector, supporting projects at all of the NASA Centers. He has taught for the graduate Engineering Science and Computer Science Departments at Loyola University in Maryland, and teaches Embedded Systems for the Johns Hopkins University, Whiting School of Engineering, Engineering for Professionals Program, and for Capitol Technology University. At Capitol, in the Summer's of 2015 and 2016, he taught Cubesat Engineering and Cubesat Operations courses.

What is an Embedded system?

First, we need to define an embedded system. Embedded computing refers to special purpose computers that are a part of a larger system, as opposed to generic desktop computers, tablets, and servers. Embedded systems are for specific purposes; they are not necessarily general purpose. They may have a limited or no human interface, but usually support complex I/O. They form the basis of all modern technical devices.

The embedded computer can be characterized by the parameters of its central processing unit (CPU), memory, and input/output (I/O). The CPU parameters of importance are speed, power consumption, word size, and price. The memory parameters include power consumption, volatility, and size or capacity. I/O characteristics must be matched to those of external systems components.

I am assuming here that the reader is generally knowledgeable about how computers work, how instructions are executed, and Input-output is accomplished. There are many good books on these topics, some of which I included in the references.

The trend now is to include more than one CPU on the chip, called Multicore technology. In addition, specialized processor units for floating point, vector processing, and digital signal processing are included. Multicore changes the game.

Embedded systems have elements of hardware and software, and these are brought together into a working system. The systems engineering process, from requirements to testing and post-deployment support is discussed. There are known approaches that work. Software is a different animal than hardware, but the top-level principles for developing and testing derive from the same principles. Programmable hardware, in terms of FPGA's and SoC's introduce more complexity, but can be addressed by the same engineering best practices.

Embedded systems have their own set of standards, and their own unique issues in security, but an embedded computer is also a computer. Virtualization and multicore technology have added new capabilities to embedded systems.

Many embedded systems are required to be real-time - they have strict deadlines. Others are event-driven - a trigger event kicks off a predetermined sequence of responses. Embedded systems are almost always resource constrained. The resources might be size, weight, power, throughput, heat generation, reliability, deadlines, etc. Embedded systems have a high non-recurring engineering (NRE) cost (development cost), but are generally cheap to produce in volume. Radiation tolerant units are much more expensive than their corresponding commercial grade units.

Embedded computer systems are constructed from monolithic microprocessor chips. Modern embedded systems might be Field Programmable Gate Array (FPGA)-based, or use a custom Application Specific Integrated Circuit (ASIC). Commodity pc boards can also form the basis of embedded system. It's just that embedded systems don't usually need or can take advantage of all the bells and whistles included with low-cost, mass-manufactured desktop computer boards.

Embedded systems can be found everywhere: refrigerators, the Space Shuttle, elevators, toothbrushes, vacuum cleaners, smartphones, automobiles, aircraft, running shoes, sewing machines, pacemakers, and more. There are a lot more embedded computers than general-purpose desktop, tablet, and server pc's. They are just sometimes harder to find.

The embedded computer can be characterized by the parameters of its central processing unit (CPU), memory, and input/output (I/O). The CPU parameters of importance are speed, power consumption, word size, and price. The memory parameters include power consumption, volatility, and size or capacity. I/O characteristics must be matched to external systems components.

Embedded processors

Very-low-cost, high-performance microprocessor-based embedded systems enable wide applications. Most of these boards, complete 32-bit computers with memory and I/O, cost less than $25. Add-on boards provide GPS location finding, wifi and bluetooth connectivity, 3-axis gyros, etc.

Advances driven by cellular phones and data systems have made available small powerful processors that rival a datacenter of a few years back. They are designed for communication, and include a variety of standard interfaces. The devices are multicore, meaning there is more than one cpu. They can include specialty cores such as floating point or digital signal processing, They have memory integrated with the cpu. They support analog as well as digital interfaces. The boards tend of be deck-of-cards size or smaller, Some examples include Arduino, Raspberry Pi, Edison, and BeagleBone boards.

Embedded microcontrollers have the cpu (or cpu's), memory, and I/O integrated onto one monolithic chip.

Software we don't need to worry so much about – if the hardware is functional, the software is generally happy. It may be difficult to debug or update the software in an extreme environment, but its been done.

What are the concerns in Embedded Systems in any environment? – security, reliability, power, data communication.

Security

All embedded systems have aspects of security. Some of these issues are addressed by existing protocols and standards for access and communications security. Security may also imply system stability and availability. Standard security measures such as security reviews and audits, threat analyses, target and threat assessments, countermeasures deployment, and extensive testing

7

apply to the embedded domain.

A security assessment of a system involves threat analysis, target assessment, risk assessment, countermeasures assessment, and testing. This is above and beyond basic system functionality.

The completed functional system may need additional security features, such as intrusion detection, data encryption, and perhaps a self-destruct capability. Is that self-destruct capability secure, so not just anyone can activate it? All of these additional features use time, space, and other resources that are usually scarce in embedded systems.

Virus and malware attacks on desktops and servers are common, and an entire industry related to detection, prevention, and correction has been spawned. These issues are not as well addressed in the embedded world. Attacks on new technology such as cell phones, tablets, and GPS systems are emerging. Not all of the threats come from individuals. Some are large government-funded efforts or commercial entities seeking proprietary information or market position. Security breaches can be inspired by ideology, money, or fame considerations. The *CERT* (Computer Emergency Response Team) organization at Carnegie Mellon University, and the *SANS* Institute (SysAdmin, Audit, Networking, and Security) track security incidents.

Techniques such as hard checksums and serial numbers are one approach to device protection. Access to the system needs to be controlled. If unused ports exist, the corresponding device drivers should be disabled, or not included. Mechanisms built into the cpu hardware can provide protection of system resources such as memory.

Security has to be designed in from the very beginning; it can't just be added on. Memorize this. There will be a quiz.

Even the most innocuous embedded platform can be used as a

springboard to penetrate other systems. It is essential to consider security of all embedded systems, be aware of industry best practices and lessons learned, and use professional help in this specialized area.

The first detection of *backdoor code* in a military grade FPGA came in May of 2012. This was detected in an Actel ProASIC3 chip. It was built into the silicon and was activated by a secret key code. This caused much distress worldwide in the FPGA/ASIC world, and for their military customers. Although this was the first detected instance of this security breach, it was probably not the first instance. We can expect more of this type of behavior in the future of embedded systems anywhere.

Reliability

What we're discussing here are systems that will be difficult or impossible to troubleshoot, repair, or retrieve. Some are on a one-way journey. We want to make them as reliable as possible. This means we do careful parts selection, careful assembly and interconnect, good mechanical engineering practices.

Software reliability is a component of System reliability. Software can be a very complex system, and needs to be addressed accordingly. Software depends on the proper operation of the hardware it is running on. By itself, software does not degrade with age or wear out. The American National Standards Institute (ANSI) defines software reliability as "the probability of failure-free operation for a specified period of time in a specified environment." As opposed to hardware, software does not wear out as a function of time. We need to define what reliability means for our specific case – 100% up time; recovery in 18 mSec? We also need to define the minimal functionality required, which might be accomplished in a fall-back mode. We also need to know how long the system has to operate. We should also consider, that when it does fail, it degrades gracefully, or fails in a safe mode.

What are the software failure mechanisms? Most software failures are related to design faults, not found in testing. There can also be a failure or ambiguity in requirements, leading to a misinterpretation. The code may be written wrong; it may have a typo. Human factors directly software correctness, defects, and reliability. This means we must have a solid system engineering approach to software development and testing. There is no good way to measure software reliability. We can say that reliability is rated (inversely) to complexity, and one measure of complexity is lines of code or logic cells. It's not a good measure, but its easy to do.

Industry standards for process, such as ISO-9000, can be applied to the software development and testing process.

Power Concerns, and the Cost of Computation

Generally, the computer data system can be designed to minimize the amount of power it consumes. The next issue is to control the amount of power the software takes.

Power is a constrained resource onboard the spacecraft, and must be carefully managed. We generally have rechargeable batteries, and solar arrays for a power source. The computer has to monitor and control the state-of-charge of the batteries, sometimes dropping everything it is doing to charge the batteries.

We also have to consider the power usage of the computer, while executing programs. Most embedded systems have some power saving modes, that come in handy for your cellphone, for example. These modes have names like "sleep" and "standby." The manufacturers' data sheet will define these modes, and their power consumption, compared to normal operation. In addition, some computers can selectively shut down some memory or I/O resources to reduce power as well.

To control power usage, we first need to add instrumentation to measure it. The embedded processor needs to be able to monitor its own power consumption.

Let's look at a simple example of onboard data processing on a cubesat imaging mission. Here we are taking consecutive images at a resolution of 5 megapixels. This is 40 megabits, at 8 bits per pixel. In Cubesats, you have a limited downlink bandwidth due to power issues, and you only have communications over land. Cubesat generally do not have the resources to utilize the Tracking and Data Relay Satellites at a higher orbit. This implies we need to know when we are over land. There are lots of ways to do this, but we could run a simple orbit model onboard with stored maps. The spacecraft takes images continuously, stores them onboard, and downlinks them when a receiver is available. We have done the trade studies, and sized the bulk storage appropriately.

We could also consider doing some image processing onboard. The Raspberry Pi, Model B 2, for example has an Image Processing pipeline separate from the main cpu cores. It is supported by an open source image processing library. We can implement various levels of data compressing on the image, or do image differencing, or process to only include "areas of interest." All of this is feasible, but involves a lot of computation, which, in turn, uses a lot of power. So, we might consider only doing the computations, on stored data, when the cubesat is in sunlight. Again, we can predict this, and it is relatively easy to sense.

We might run into a conflict between processing the images, and downlinking them, if the cubesat is in sunlight, and over land. To see if any of this makes sense, we have to instrument the computer to measure its power consumption. Typically, a housekeeping task for an onboard computer is to keep track of the state-of-charge of the battery's by measuring current in and current out.

On the test bench, we can establish the energy required to process an image, and the energy needed to downlink it. From this data, we can decide the correct approach to apply. What we have measured and computed is the energy cost of computation.

Standards

There are many Standards applicable to embedded systems. These range from general computer standards to embedded-specific embedded standards. Why should we be interested in standards? Standards represent an established approach, based on best practices. Standards are not created to stifle creativity or direct an implementation approach, but rather to give the benefit of previous experience. Adherence to standards implies that different parts will work together. Standards are often developed by a single company, and then adopted by the relevant industry. Other Standards are imposed by large customer organizations such as the Department of Defense, or the automobile industry. Many standards organizations exist to develop, review, and maintain standards.

Standards exist in many areas, including hardware, software, interfaces, protocols, testing, system safety, security, and certification. Standards can be open or closed (proprietary). Sometimes, the embedded systems customer will insist on adherence to specified standards.

Hardware standards include the form factor and packaging of chips, the electrical interface, the bus interface, the power interface, and others. The JTAG standard specifies an interface for debugging.

In computer architecture, the ISA specifies the instruction set and the operations. It does not specify the implementation. Popular ISA's are x86 (Intel) and ARM (ARM Holdings, LTD). These are proprietary, and licensed by the Intellectual Property holder.

In software, an API (applications program interface) specifies the interface between a user program, and the operating system. To run properly, the program must adhere to the API. POSIX is an IEEE standard for portable operating systems.

There are numerous Quality standards, such as those from ISO, and Carnegie-Mellon's CMM (Capability Maturity Model). CMM defines five levels of organizational maturity in a company or institution, and is independently audited.

Language standards also exist, such as those for the ANSI c and Java languages. Networking standards include TCP/IP for Ethernet, the CAN bus from Bosch, and IEEE-1553 for avionics.

The ISO-9000 standard was developed by the International Standards Organization, and applies to a broad range industries. It concentrates on process. It's validation is based on extensive documentation of organization's process in a particular area, such as software development, system build, system integration, and test and certification. It is always good to review what standards are and could be applied to an embedded system, as it ensures the application of best practices from experience, and interoperability with other systems.

The Portable Operating System Interface for Unix (POSIX) is an IEEE standard, IEEE 1003.1-1988. The standard spans some 17 documents. POSIX provides a Unix-like environment and API. Various operating systems are certified to POSIX compliance, including BSD, LynxOS, QNX, VxWorks, and others.

ARINC 653 is a software specification (API) for space and time partitioning in safety critical real-time operating systems. Each piece of application software has its own memory and dedicated time slot. The specification dates from 1996.

Mobile platforms

Many standard tracked, wheeled, and legged platforms are available to get our system to the extremes, as well as conventional model aircraft and rotating wing aircraft on the Quad-copter pattern. Many radio-controlled models, boats, submersibles, electric aircraft, cars, and trucks are readily available and inexpensive. A walking platform is feasible, but more complex. These serve as the mobility platforms for integrating computational, sensor, and communication packages. These might be adequate for the job, or at least the proof-of-concept prototype. This is another area where you don't have to (literally) reinvent the wheel.

Actuators such as motors can themselves have built-in embedded computers. These are referred to as smart actuators. They may incorporate a local feedback and monitoring loop. IEEE-1451 is a set of standards for interfacing smart sensors and smart actuators. The standards cover functions, communication protocols, and formats.

Flight Platforms

Flight platforms come in several configurations. The lighter than air craft include balloon payloads, and aerostats, or blimps. For heavier than air craft, the choices are fixed wing, and rotary wing. Big advances have been made in small rotary wing craft, leading to the 4-bladed hex copter, and 6-rotor devices. The rotors can be tilted individually for attitude control, or in combination, for vertical or horizontal flight. The advantage of winged craft is that they can glide. Kite-borne payloads can also be used, but they are mostly at the mercy of the winds.

Advanced battery and motor technology

Batteries have gotten better, due to new applications in hybrid and full-electric cars, small electric aircraft and boats, and cell phones.

Rechargeable batteries in new chemistries are also the outgrowth of hybrid and full electric vehicles. The energy density is very high. Technologies like lithium-polymer (LioP) have created expanded the operating life of equipment before recharging is required, and allowed for solar recharge. These types of batteries were in consumer electronics by 1995.

They also have the advantage of being lightweight. They also provide a higher discharge rate (greater current) than other battery technologies. However, overcharge, over discharge, and penetration can result in explosion. Special charging circuits are required, as well as temperature and discharge current monitoring.

Open Source versus Proprietary

This is a topic we need to discuss before we get very far into software. It is not a technical topic, but concerns your right to use (and/or own, modify) software. It's those software licenses you click to agree with, and never read. That's what the intellectual property lawyers are betting on.

Software and software tools are available in proprietary and open source versions. Open source software is free and widely available, and may be incorporated into your system. It is available under license, which generally says that you can use it, but derivative products must be made available under the same license. This presents a problem if it is mixed with purchased, licensed commercial software, or a level of exclusivity is required. Major government agencies such as the Department of Defense and NASA have policies related to the use of Open Source software.

Adapting a commercial or open source operating system to a particular problem domain can be tricky. Usually, the commercial operating systems need to be used "as-is" and the source code is not available. The software can usually be configured between well-defined limits, but there will be no visibility of the internal workings. For the open source situation, there will be a multitude of source code modules and libraries that can be configured and customized, but the process is complex. The user can also write new modules in this case.

Large corporations or government agencies sometimes have problems incorporating open source products into their projects. Open Source did not fit the model of how they have done business traditionally. They are issues and lingering doubts. Many Federal agencies have developed Open Source policies. NASA has created an open source license, the NASA Open Source Agreement (NOSA), to address these issues. It has released software under this license, but the Free Software Foundation had some issues with the terms of the license. The Open Source Initiative (www.opensource.org) maintains the definition of Open Source, and certifies licenses such as the NOSA.

The GNU General Public License (GPL) is the most widely used free software license. It guarantees end users the freedoms to use, study, share, copy, and modify the software. Software that ensures that these rights are retained is called free software. The license was originally written by Richard Stallman of the Free Software Foundation (FSF) for the GNU project in 1989. The GPL is a *copyleft* license, which means that derived works can only be distributed under the same license terms. This is in distinction to permissive free software licenses, of which the BSD licenses are the standard examples. Copyleft is in counterpoint to traditional copyright. Proprietary software "poisons" free software, and cannot be included or integrated with it, without abandoned the GPL. The GPL covers the GNU/linux operating systems and most of the GNU/linux-based applications.

A Vendor's software tools and operating system or application code is usually proprietary intellectual property. It is unusual to get the source code to examine, at least without binding legal documents and additional funds. Along with this, you do get the vendor support. An alternative is open source code, which is in the public domain. There are a series of licenses covering open source code usage, including the Creative Commons License, the gnu public license, copyleft, and others. Open Source describes a collaborative environment for development and testing. Use of open source code carries with it an implied responsibility to "pay back" to the community. Open Source is not necessarily free.

The Open source philosophy is sometimes at odds with the rigidized procedures evolved to ensure software performance and reliability. Offsetting this is the increased visibility into the internals of the software packages, and control over the entire software package. Besides application code, operating systems such as GNU/linux and bsd can be open source. The programming language Python is open source. The popular web server Apache is also open source.

An Architectural Model

This section discusses an architectural model for embedded systems, hardware and software, operating in extreme environments.

NASREM

The NASA/NBS Standard Reference Model for Telerobot Control System Architecture was evolved as a model for the implementation of advanced control architectures.

The NBS architecture is a generic framework in which to implement intelligence of a telerobotic device. It was developed over a decade as part of a research program in industrial robotics at NBS (now. NIST) in which over $25 million was spent. The NBS program involved over fifty professionals and extensive facilities, including robots, a supercomputer, mainframes. minicomputers. microcomputers. LISP machines. and AI workstations. This model, designed originally for industrial robots. is the mechanism by which sensors. expert systems. and controls are linked and operated such that a system behaves with some measure of autonomy, if

17

not intelligence.

Systems designed from this model perform complex real-time tasks in the presence of sensory input from a variety of sensors. They decomposes high level goals into low level actions. making real-time decisions in the presence of noise and conflicting demands on resources. The model provides a framework for linking artificial intelligence. expert system. and neural techniques with classical real-time control. Sensors are interfaced to controls through a hierarchically-structured real-time world model. The world model integrates current sensory data with a priori knowledge to provide the control system with a current best estimate of the state of the system.

NASREM is a generic hierarchical structured functional model for the overall system. The hierarchical nature makes it ideal for telerobot systems, and for gradual evolution of the system. The model also provides a set of common reference terminology, which can enable the construction of a database. It defines interfaces, which allows for modularization. The model allows for evolutionary growth, while providing a structure of the interleaving of human:robotic control.

NASREM's 6-level model operates from a global memory (or database). At each level we have three processes, sensory processing world modeling, and task decomposition (execute). At the very lowest level, we have the raw sensors and the servo systems. Going up from that, we have the primitive level, the elementary move level, the task level, the service bay level, and the mission level. At the servo level, we would find cameras, and their associated pan/tilt control as well as mobility and joint motor control, with associated position feedback. At the primitive move level, we would find the camera subsystem, the arm, the mobility subsystem, and the grippers. At the elementary (or e-) move level, we would find systems such as perception or manipulation. At the task level, we might locate the entire telerobotic system.

The world modeling process starts with a sparse database. Sensor data, appropriate to the level flows in, and there might be a capability for data fusion. A task planner task can make "what-if" queries of the world model (which is state-based). The modeling task uses a global database of state variable, lists, maps and knowledge bases to allow a modeling process to update and predict states, to evaluate current states and possible states, and to report results to a task executor task. The World model, evaluates states, both existing states as evidenced by sensor data, and possible states, as postulated by the task planner.

The timing and time horizon of the various levels of the model is are vastly different. The servo level operates on the millisecond level, the primitive level, at 10's to 100's of milliseconds, and the e-move level at about a one second update interval. It would have about a 30 second planning horizon. The task level would have update interval on the order of seconds to 10's of seconds, with a planning horizon in the 10's of seconds. Moving up, the service by level would update in the 1's of seconds, with a planning horizon the order of minutes to 10's of minutes. Finally, the mission level might update on the order of minutes, with a horizon of an hour.

The servo level would accept Cartesian trajectory points from the next level up, and transform these to drive voltages or current for the mechanisms. The Primitive level would accept pose (or collection of joint angles and positions) information from the next higher level, and generate the Cartesian trajectory point to pass down the hierarchy. These involve dynamics calculations. The e-move level would accept elementary move commands and generate pose commands, after orientations in the coordinate frame, singularities, and clearances. It uses simple if-then state transition rules. The task level, the one the telerobot would be located at, accepts task commands (from the human operator), does subsystem assignments and scheduling, and generates a series of e-moves.

Real Time Control System (RCS)

RCS evolved form NASREM over decades, starting in the 1970's It is currently at RCS Level 4. RCS is a Reference Model Architecture for real-time control. It provides a framework for implementation in terms of a hierarchical control model derived from best theory and best practices. RCS was heavily influenced by the understanding of the biological cerebellum. NIST maintains a library of RCS software listings, scripts and tools, in ADA, Java, and C++.

An abstraction, the perfect joint accepts analog or digital torque commands, and produces the required torque via a dc motor. It also provides state feedback in the form of force, torque, angle or position, (depending on whether the joint configuration is Cartesian or revolute), and possibly rate. The perfect joint includes a pulse width modulator (pwm), a motor, and possibly a gearbox. Internal feedback and compensation is provided to compensate for gearbox or other irregularities such as hysteresis or stiction, For example, the torque pulses common to harmonic drives can be compensated for within the perfect joint. The perfect joint is part of the lowest NASREM level. The processing provided theoretically achieves a "perfect" torque, where the outputted torque matches the commanded torque.

The Individual Joint Controller (IJC) implements a simple control law to allow joint by joint operation of the manipulator.

The IJC provides a functional redundancy to the higher level telerobot control. It accepts inputs from a kinematically similar mini-master controller. This simplifies the computational requirements on the IJC, by removing the need for coordinate transformations. The IJC does not include any dynamic joint coupling compensation. It basically implements seven parallel, non-interacting control laws, that may be simple PD loops.

A telerobot control system can be implemented the first 3 (of 7) levels of the NASREM model. Further levels could be added later in a phased evolution of the system. For early systems, the human operator provided the functionality of the upper control levels.

The telerobot controller initially implemented the first three NAS-REM levels, and could accept commands from a joystick-type element, a mini-master, or higher levels of the model. This level required a computational capability of several MIPS, and an accuracy of 32 bits. Floating point capability was assumed. This controller could perform coordinate transformations in real time, although the computation burden argued for a custom hardware approach to this particular subset of the computations.

Security

You don't want to enable a situation in which some one else takes over your remote system. Design the system so this can't happen.

All embedded systems have aspects of security. Embedded systems on robots operate in an unfriendly world. They are vulnerable to variations of hacking, viruses and malware, theft, damage, spoofing, and other nasty techniques from the desktop/server world. GPS systems can be hacked to provide incorrect location or critical time information. Cell phones and tablets are connected wirelessly to large networks. A bored teenage hacker in Europe took over the city Tram system as his private full-scale railroad, using a TV remote. What about the teenager in an internet café is a third-world country. Can he take over and play with your robot?

Some of these issues are addressed by existing protocols and standards for access and communications security. Security may also imply system stability and availability. Standard security measures such as security reviews and audits, threat analyses, target and threat assessments, countermeasures deployment, and extensive testing apply to the embedded domain.

A security assessment of a system involves threat analysis, target assessment, risk assessment, countermeasures assessment, and testing. This is above and beyond basic system functionality.

The completed functional system may need additional security features, such as intrusion detection, data encryption, and perhaps a self-destruct capability. Is that self-destruct capability secure, so not just anyone can activate it? All of these additional features use time, space, and other resources that are usually scarce in embedded systems.

Virus and malware attacks on desktops and servers are common, and an entire industry related to detection, prevention, and correction has been spawned. These issues are not as well addressed in the embedded world. Attacks on new technology such as cell phones, pda's, tablets, and GPS systems are emerging. Not all of the threats come from individuals. Some are large government-funded efforts or commercial entities seeking proprietary information or market position. Security breaches can be inspired by ideology, money, or fame considerations. The *CERT* (Computer Emergency Response Team) organization at Carnegie Mellon University, and the *SANS Institute* (SysAdmin, Audit, Networking, and Security) track security incidents.

Techniques such as hard checksums and serial numbers are one approach to device protection. Access to the system needs to be controlled. If unused ports exist, the corresponding device drivers should be disabled, or not included. Mechanisms built into the cpu hardware can provide protection of system resources such as memory.

Security has to be designed in from the very beginning; it can't just be added on. Memorize this. There will be a quiz.

Even the most innocuous embedded platform can be used as a springboard to penetrate other systems. It is essential to consider security of all embedded systems, be aware of industry best practices and lessons learned, and use professional help in this specialized area.

Testing

Testing the system in the target environment is another challenge. Sometimes it is difficult to duplicate the environment in a laboratory setting. It may involve a large thermal vacuum chamber. Usually, the parts, boards, and boxes are tested before the integrated assembly is tested. Mobility systems present another challenge.

At the Jet Propulsion Lab, they deploy the Mars rovers in an area with similar geology to that planet.. But the air pressure and temperature is Earth normal, and the gravity is wrong.

It is important to understand the target environment, and test components, boards, boxes, and assemblies for the environment they will face operationally.

When I was working on the Greenland Rover Project for NASA, I told the student designers that if it failed, they would be dropped on the ice sheet with a voltmeter and a screwdriver, and we'd pick them up when it was working again. We got a very reliable design and implementation, with a lot of self-monitoring.

Self-monitoring and cross monitoring

Homeostasis refers to a system that monitors, corrects, and controls its own state. Our bodies do that with our blood pressure, temperature, blood sugar level, and many other parameters.

We can have the embedded processor monitor its performance, or have two identical systems monitor each other. Each approach has problems. We can also choose to "triplicate" the hardware, and use external logic to see if results differ. The idea is, two outweigh one, because the probability of a double error is less than that of a single error.

In at least one case I know of, the backup computer erroneously thought the primary machine made a mistake, and took over control. It was wrong, and caused a system failure.

To counter the effects of "bit flips" and other effects of radiation, the memory can be designed with error detection and correction (EDAC). Generally, this means a longer, encoded word that can detect n and correct M errors. There is a trade-off with price. With EDAC memory, there is a low priority background task running on the cpu that continuously reading and writing back to memory. This process, called "memory scrubbing" will catch and correct errors.

Self-test software can be included, usually running as a background task. This might also send a "heart-beat" signal to another processor or logic. At the hardware level, particularly if we are using configurable logic, we can include built-in self test (BIST).

A special-purpose timer essential for embedded applications is the Watchdog. This is a free-running timer that generates a cpu reset unless it is reset by the software. This helps to ensure that the system doesn't lock up during certain critical time periods, and the software is meeting its deadlines. This approach has saved many a system.

If the watchdog is not reset, it generates an interrupt to reset the host. This should take the system back to a baseline state, and restart it. Hopefully, normal operations will resume. The embedded system can't rely on a human operator to notice a fault in the operations or a "hung" system, and press the reset button. Many *very remote* systems, such as those in deep water or on the surface of other planets have successfully recovered from faults with a watchdog.

The watchdog timer is implemented in hardware, and does it's jobs without direct software intervention. If the software fails to reset the timer, the system reboots. This might simply reset operations and restart, or may include diagnostics before the system is restarted. So, who watches the watchdog?

Harsh and Extreme Environments

This section, from Wikipedia, lists a series of extreme

environments. We might need to address any of these with an embedded system. Among extreme environments are alkaline, acidic, extremely cold, extremely hot, hyper-saline, places without water or oxygen, and places altered by humans, such as mine tailings or oil impacted habitats. That's on this planet. This is a good working set of definitions:

- *Alkaline* is an environment with a pH above 9.

- *Acidic* is an environment with a pH less than 5.

- *Extremely cold* is an environment with a temperature below -17°C. Examples include polar sites and deep ocean habitats. The main challenge in implementing systems for the cold environment is finding components for low-temp use. There exists no large market for them, so most companies don't specify or test components for very low temperatures.

- *Extremely hot* is an environment with a temperature above 40°C. Examples would be geological areas such as found in Yellowstone Park or deep-sea vents. The Definitions for very low and high temperature ranges is:

Low-Temperature −55°C/−65°C
Cryogenic −150°C (T < 120 K
High-Temperature > +125°C
Wide-Temperature <−55°C/−65°C to +125°C or greater

- Hypersaline: environments that have salt concentrations greater than that of seawater, or >3.5%. This includes salt lakes. The type of salt may alos be importand

- Under pressure refers to environments under extreme hydrostatic pressure such as aquatic habitats deeper than 2000 meters and enclosed habitats under pressure.

- Radiation refers to areas exposed to abnormally high radiation or of radiation outside the normal range of light (high UV or IR radiation)

- Environments without free water includes both hot and cold desert environments, and certain endolithic habitats. An endolith is an organism that lives within rock.

- Environments without oxygen includes habitats in deeper sediments.

- Environments altered by humans includes mine tailings, oil impacted habitats, and pollution by heavy metals or organic compounds.

Keep in mind, an environment our system has to operate in can have more than one of these characteristics simultaneously. On Earth, we have fresh and salt water environments, with the issue of pressure as we go deeper. Go deep enough, and you'll encounter the geothermal vents, spewing forth high temperature water under great pressure. The water is generally infused with minerals and contaminants such as mercury.

Domains

Embedded electronics can operate in many domains. With difficulty, they can be designed to operate in two very different domains. This section will discuss the unique challenges of the different terrestrial environments.

Ground

Ground based robot explorers can use a variety of locomotion. This includes wheels, treads, legs, etc. The Mars rovers tend to be 6 wheel vehicles, with each wheel operating independently under computer control. Legged locomotion is more complex to accomplish, but is more versatile in rough terrain. Hovercraft can be used, but they expend a lot of energy getting and staying airborne. They work well over ice, which is generally smooth, but not over sandy areas, where they create their own dust cloud. Wheeled systems are the simplest and easiest, although tracks are called for in difficult terrain. It is less energy efficient. Many wheeled, tracked, and legged platforms are available in the marketplace.. Larger platforms can use re-purposed internal-combustion powered vehicles. The larger the chassis, the more the need for built-in safety. Take this from a guy who was pinned to the wall by a 600 pound mobile platform, without the big red stop-now button in reach.

Underground

The underground environment is challenging as well. We have to reach it through a natural or man-made opening – examples are caves, lava tubes, and mines. The environment might be water-filled, presenting another set of challenges. Communications is also a challenge, and dragging a tether is usually not feasible.

We should also consider a water environment under ice. This is common in the Polar regions, and may be present on some of the moons of Jupiter and Saturn. Not much is know about the interface region between sea ice and the deeper saline water. There may or may not be an air layer under the ice. The salt water environment is corrosive to metals. Orientation is difficult.

The drilling industry is a major one, harvesting oil and gas, and geothermal fluids, as well as drinking water. Those man-made holes in the ground employ some interesting technologies.

The temperature of the earth's crust increases downward at about 30°C per kilometer. The pressures created by the weight of overlying rocks also increase significantly with increasing depth. The pressure in the rocks goes up by 300 bars per kilometer increase in depth. A system in a tunnel would not experience this pressure directly, as the pressure in the air in the tunnel is only affected by the weight of the air above. Air pressure goes up with depth, but slowly. But, as the rock pressure goes up, the walls of a tunnel are subjected to larger forces, which can lead to partial collapse of tunnel walls or ceilings (called rock bursts). Rock bursts and tunnel stability become important problems at depths of several kilometers and are well known in deep mines.

If the engineering problems are overcome, a more fundamental lower limit of tunnel depth is imposed by a change in the physical properties of rocks, which occurs from about 10 to 20 km depth, depending on local conditions and rock type. At those depths, rocks begin to flow plastically, like taffy, and any opening would slowly squeeze shut. The flow is temperature-sensitive very slow at the top of the plastic zone (about 350 C), but become faster as temperature increases.

Desert

The desert environment is harsh in different ways. It represents the extremes of temperatures, and usually consists of sand, which can act as a fluid under the right conditions, making surface mobility difficult. On the other hand, you can surf down some sand dunes. With little or no vegetation, winds are harsh. The temperatures at night plummet to extreme lows. Blown sand can cover and effectively disable solar panels (this has been observed on Mars.)

28

Air

Flying explorers can cover a lot of ground, with an increase in the energy expended. Winged systems can glide, minimizing energy expenditure. Winged craft have found no off-planet applications so far. First, you need an atmosphere (rules out the moon), and enough atmosphere (makes Mars difficult). Balloon-borne payloads have been proposed for Jupiter, which, as far as we know, has no solid surface. For low altitude and short to moderate duration missions, the quad-copter or hex copter configuration is good. The energy expenditure is high, and they are not quiet.

Lighter-than-air systems typically use helium for the lift. The are usually vertical systems, and they are at the mercy of the winds. Tethered balloon or aerostats can also be used. Very high altitude balloon platforms can reach the fringes of space. Balloons are subject to wind drift. Aerostats can remain airborne for months.

Flying through Hurricanes is routinely done by a dedicated cadre of pilots and crew, operating from southern Florida. The in-situ measurements they provide are invaluable to tracking and early warning of these storms. It is also incredibly dangerous. NOAA is now using unmanned instrumented drones in this role. They are expendable, have a longer working time on target, and provide more data. These units may eliminate or minimize the hazards of manned missions. Five aircrew have been lost in hurricane hunter missions since they started in 1943. A safer alternative, unmanned aircraft have evolved to where they are being tested in this role. This was spurred by the need for further real-time data on Hurricane Sandy in 2012.

NASA and NOAA has an active program, using their two Global Hawks. The Global Hawk is launched from the ground, and can achieve an altitude of 60,000 feet, and a flight duration of 24 hours. The aircraft has a turbofan engine, and a payload capacity of 2,000 pounds.

NOAA is also using the smaller Coyote drone. These unmanned

aircraft are three feet long and between 12 and 14 pounds. They can carry either electro-optical or infrared cameras and data transmitter payloads. They can achieve between 60 and 85 knots and a ceiling of 20,000 feet. They have a six-foot wingspan, and are deployed from an aircraft in flight.

In 2014, NOAA dropped four Coyote drones directly into the eye and surrounding eye wall of Hurricane Edouard, providing scientists with continuous pressure, temperature, wind and humidity data from the critical part of the storm

Water/underwater

Water-based systems can be limited to the surface, or can be designed for sub-surface operations as well.

Smart buoys, floating data platforms, can be tethered or drifting. Vast networks of smart drifting buoys are returning data on currents, ocean temperature and salinity, and other data for that ¾ of the planet we don't have complete data for. They are generally solar powered.

I worked on smart buoys for the Coast Guard. You know what their major problem is? Not computation, not communication, not sensors – bird poop. Buoys are out there all alone on a flat watery surface, and provide a nice resting point for birds, who, unfortunately leave behind a material that hardens to concrete-like properties, and requires a grinder to remove. This is the major technological hurdle to more smart buoys.

For submersibles, the farther you go down, the more the pressure increases, and the greater the problem in keeping the water out of the vehicle. That having been said, submersibles have been to the deepest part of the ocean, and imaged weird life forms that thrive on volcanic vents. The farther you want to go down, the more expensive it is going to be. Platforms tend to be very specialized. The oil industry is a major customer for the commercial units, ROV's, or remotely operated vehicles, with grippers and arms. We would say, telerobot.

There is an interesting open source project called OpenROV that involves a do-it-yourself fairly low cost telerobot underwater explorer. I would like someone in Australia to put a couple of these at the Great Barrier Reef, and allow teleoperation via the Internet.

Mono Lake, located in California's Eastern Sierra, is both an alkaline and hypersaline environment. Octopus Spring is a partially alkaline, low-carbonate, low-sulfur hot spring located in the Lower Geyser Basin of Yellowstone National Park. It is home to a variety of thermophiles, showing the diversity of life. Water temperature at the source is about 95 degrees C.

Deep in the Earth

The TauTona gold mine in Africa runs about 55deg c ambient (which is life-threating) at 3.9 km underground, which is about the limit for humans to work. It is not pleasant.

Altered by human activity

The Rio Tinto is an extremely acidic (ph 2.0) river in southern Spain. Enduring over 5000 years of mining activity, the river is full of heavy metals. It originates in the mountains of Andulasia, and drains into the Gulf of Cadiz. It actually supports a surprising diversity of adapted life forms. It is being used by NASA to plan future Mars missions in similar environments.

Nuclear Plants

There have been at least three major incidents in nuclear power plants, in which teleoperated robotic devices were used to aid in reconnaissance. The United States, Russia, and Japan all found need of these alternatives to humans. Unfortunately, the electronics on the robots are as susceptible to radiation as human tissue. But we can build more robots, and use out knowledge of radiation hardening to make them last longer.

Chernobyl

In 1986, there was a disaster at the Chernobyl Nuclear Plant in the Ukraine, then part of the Soviet Union. The major problem was the collapsed roof of the reactor. The first responders were mostly killed, either immediately or died shortly after. The remote-controlled bulldozers obtained from East Germany proved too heavy. Human workers in the area were limited to 90 seconds of total lifetime exposure, in which they could not get a lot done.

A French documentary, *Tank on the Moon*, presents a solution in which the original Lunokhod designers were called back from retirement, and used their already-radiation hardened electronics to duplicate the lunar design. These rovers, called STR-1's, were deployed to clear debris, and document the damage. They still eventually failed due to cumulative radiation damage to the electronics, but were useful for some time.

Interestingly, robots sent inside the facility later, discovered a new form of fungi, thriving in the high radiation environment. Samples were obtained, and its properties were studied.

"This slime, a collection of several fungi actually, was more than just surviving in a radioactive environment, it was actually using gamma radiation as a food source. Samples of these fungi grew significantly faster when exposed to gamma radiation at 500 times the normal background radiation level. The fungi appear to use melanin, a chemical found in human skin as well, in the same fashion as plants use chlorophyll. That is to say, the melanin molecule gets struck by a gamma ray and its chemistry is altered. This is an *amazing* discovery, no one had even suspected that something like this was possible." Weird life forms on our planet makes you wonder what else is out there. These are referred to as extremophiles.

Three Mile Island

To quote from Wikipedia, "Three Mile Island Nuclear Generating Station (TMI) is a nuclear power plant (NPP) located on Three Mile Island in the Susquehanna River, south of Harrisburg, Pennsylvania in Londonderry Township. It has two separate units, known as TMI-1 and TMI-2. The plant is widely known for having been the site of the most significant accident in United States commercial nuclear energy, on March 28, 1979, when TMI-2 suffered a partial meltdown. According to the US Nuclear Regulatory Commission, the accident resulted in no deaths or injuries to plant workers or members of nearby communities."

"In March of the same year Red Whittaker received his Ph. D., the nuclear reactor at nearby Three Mile Island nearly experienced a meltdown. Within a budget of $1.5 million, Whittaker and his colleagues at Carnegie Mellon built robots to inspect and perform repairs in the reactor's damaged basement, and their experiences with that project resulted in the creation of the Field Robotics Center at Carnegie Mellon University. Whittaker's later teams would also develop robots to help with the aftermath of the nuclear reactor accident at Chernobyl in 1986. In 1987, Whittaker co-founded RedZone Robotics to develop and sell (or lease) robots that could operate in hazardous environments and situations too dangerous for humans."

Inside the human body

Well, it can't be too bad, but implantable medical devices have to cope with our internal environment, while not posing any risks to the host. These devices include pacemakers for the heart, and drug injection systems. There are problems with thermal management, energy management, and dialectic issues. Universities with strong Electrical Engineering, Computer Science, and Medical Schools are driving this technology. Safety is a primary requirement.

Inside the car

Automotive applications of embedded systems as a market has exploded. Embedded automotive processors can be found in airbag/crash systems, roll-over and stability control, engine control and monitoring, transmission control and monitoring, *infotainment* systems, driver assist systems, and systems monitoring and management. Hybrid (gas-electric) vehicles feature advanced battery management, "fuel state" calculation, and powertrain control. Cars can park themselves now, and self-driving cars are appearing. It is no longer a technology issue, but a regulatory and legal one.

Automobiles have used microprocessor-based controllers since the 1970's. There was a desire to reduce emissions, and simultaneously increase both fuel economy and performance. This was not going to happen with mechanical systems such as carburetors. Analog controllers were tried, but were troublesome. Then, 8-bit, and later 16-bit embedded processors used look-up tables in memory to determine the exact optimal operating time for the fuel injectors, based on multiple input parameters from engine sensors. 32-bit processors allowed for the function to be calculated in real-time, and the look-up table was no longer required.

The major problem in automotive electronics is underhood temperature. Anything that is in the cabin with the driver and passengers is in a "room" type environment, generally.

The underhood automotive environment is harsh and current trends in the automotive electronics industry are pushing the temperature envelope for electronic components. The desire to place engine control units on the engine and transmission control units either on or in the transmission pushes the ambient temperature above 125°C. However, extreme cost pressures, increasing reliability demands, and the cost of field failures make the shift to higher temperatures occur incrementally. The coolest spots on engine and in the transmission will be used. These large bodies do provide considerable heat sinking to reduce temperature rise due to power dissipation in the control unit. The majority of near term applications are 150°C or less and these will be worst case temperatures, not nominal. The transition to drive-by-wire technology, replacing mechanical and hydraulic systems with electromechanical systems, will require more power electronics. Integration of power transistors and smart power devices into the electromechanical actuator (smart actuator) requires power devices to operate at 175°C to 200°C. Hybrid electric vehicles and fuel cell vehicles also drive the demand for higher temperature power electronics. In the case of hybrid electric and fuel cell vehicles, the high temperature will be due to power dissipation. The alternates to high-temperature devices are thermal management systems which add weight and cost. The number of sensors in vehicles is increasing as more electrically controlled systems are added. Many of these sensors must work in high-temperature environments. The harshest applications are exhaust gas sensors and cylinder pressure or combustion sensors. High-temperature electronics use in automotive systems continue to grow, but will be gradual as cost and reliability issues are addressed.

From, Johnson, R. Wayne "The Changing Automotive Environment: High-Temperature Electronics." IEEE TRANSACTIONS ON ELECTRONICS PACKAGING MANUFACTURING, VOL. 27, NO. 3, JULY 2004

Space

The space environment is hostile and non-forgiving. There is little or no gravity, so no convection cooling, leading to thermal problems. It is a high radiation environment. The system is power constrained. And, it is hard to debug and repair after launch.

There are differing environments by Mission type. For Near-Earth orbiters, there are the radiation problems of the Van Allen belts and South Atlantic Anomaly, and the issue of atmospheric drag. Missions were Shuttle serviceable, as long as the Shuttle fleet was available. Synchronous or L2 (Lagrange Point) missions are not fixable, at the present time. If we go towards the sun it gets hot. That includes missions to Venus or Mercury. If we go away from the sun, it gets cold, and the amount of energy we can capture via solar arrays is limited. This includes missions to the asteroids, Mars, Jupiter, Saturn, the outer planets, and their associated moons.

Planetary Probes include orbiters, rovers, and atmospheric or surface packages. There were Mercury and Venus landers, Mars rovers and orbiters, Jovian and Saturnian moon probes, which have to deal with extreme radiation belts, and missions to the outer planets and beyond the solar system.

The functions of the embedded controllers on the spacecraft include navigation, attitude control and pointing, orbit control & maintenance, thermal control, energy management, and data management and communications (which may include antenna pointing).

Radiation Effects

There are two radiation problem areas: cumulative dose, and single event. Operating above the Van Allen belts of particles trapped in Earth's magnetic flux lines, spacecraft are exposed to the full fury of the Universe. Earth's magnetic poles do not align with the rotational poles, so the Van Allen belts dip to around 200 kilometers in the South Atlantic, leaving a region called the South Atlantic Anomaly. The magnetic field lines are good at deflecting charged particles, but mostly useless against electromagnetic radiation and uncharged particles such as neutrons. One trip across the Van Allen belts can ruin a spacecraft's electronics. Some spacecraft turn off sensitive electronics for several minutes every ninety minutes – every pass through the low dipping belts in the South Atlantic.

The Earth and other planets are constantly immersed in the solar wind, a flow of hot plasma emitted by the Sun in all directions, a result of the two-million-degree heat of the Sun's outermost layer, the Corona. The solar wind usually reaches Earth with a velocity around 400 km/s, with a density around 5 ions/cm^3. During magnetic storms on the Sun, flows can be several times faster, and stronger. The Sun tends to have an eleven year cycle of maxima. A solar flare is a large explosion in the Sun's atmosphere that can release as much as 6×10^{25} joules in one event, equal to about one sixth of the Sun's total energy output every second. Solar flares are frequently coincident with sun spots. Solar flares, being releases of large amounts of energy, can trigger Coronal Mass Ejections, and accelerate lighter particles to near the speed of light toward the planets.

The size of the Van Allen Belts shrink and expand in response to the Solar Wind. The wind is made up of particles, electrons up to 10 Million electron volts (MeV), and protons up to 100 Mev – all ionizing doses. One charged particle can knock thousands of electrons loose from the semiconductor lattice, causing noise, spikes, and current surges. Since memory elements are capacitors, they can be damaged or discharged, essentially changing state.

Vacuum tube based technology is essentially immune from radiation effects. The Russians designed (but did not complete) a Venus Rover mission using vacuum tube electronics.

Not that just current electronics are vulnerable. The Great Auroral Exhibition of 1859 interacted with the then-extant telegraph lines acting as antennae, such that batteries were not needed for the telegraph apparatus to operate for hours at a time. Some telegraph systems were set on fire, and operators shocked. The whole show is referred to as the Carrington Event, after amateur British Astronomer Richard Carrington.

Around other planets, the closer we get to the Sun, the bigger the impact of solar generated particles, and the less predictable they are. Auroras have been observed on Venus, in spite of the planet not having an observed magnetic field. The impact of the solar particles becomes less of a problem with the outer planets. Auroras have been observed on Mars, and the magnetic filed of Jupiter, Saturn, and some of the moons cause their "Van Allen belts" to trap large numbers of energetic particles, which cause more problems for spacecraft in transit. Both Jupiter and Saturn have magnetic field greater than Earth's. Not all planets have a magnetic field, so not all have charged particle belts.

Radiation Hardness Issues for Space Flight Applications

A complete discussion of the physics of radiation damage to semiconductors is beyond the scope of this document. However, an overview of the subject is presented. The tolerance of semiconductor devices to radiation must be examined in the light of their damage susceptibility. The problems fall into two broad categories, those caused by cumulative dose, and those transient events caused by asynchronous very energetic particles, such as those experienced during a period of intense solar flare activity. The unit of absorbed dose of radiation is the *rad*, representing the absorption of 100 ergs of energy per gram of material. A kilo-rad is one thousand rads. At 10k rad, death in humans is almost instantaneous. One hundred kilo-rad is typical in the vicinity of Jupiter's radiation belts. Ten to twenty kilo-rad is typical for spacecraft in low Earth orbit, but the number depends on how much time the spacecraft spends outside the Van Allen belts, which act as a shield by trapping energetic particles.

Absorbed radiation can cause temporary or permanent changes in the semiconductor material. Usually neutrons, being uncharged, do minimal damage, but energetic protons and electrons cause lattice or ionization damage in the material, and resultant parametric changes. For example, the leakage current can increase, or bit states can change. Certain technologies and manufacturing processes are known to produce devices that are less susceptible to damage than others. More expensive substrate materials such as diamond or sapphire help to make the device more tolerant of radiation, but much more expensive.

Radiation tolerance of 100 kilo-rad is usually more than adequate for low Earth orbit (LEO) missions that spend most of their life below the shielding of the Van Allen belts. For Polar missions, a higher total dose is expected, from 100k to 1 mega-rad per year. For synchronous, equatorial orbits, that are used by many communication satellites, and some weather satellites, the expected dose is several kilo-rad per year. Finally, for planetary missions to Venus, Mars, Jupiter, Saturn, and beyond, requirements that are even more stringent must be met. For one thing, the missions usually are unique, and the cost of failure is high. For missions towards the sun, the higher fluence of solar radiation must be taken into account. The larger outer planets, such as Jupiter and Saturn, have their own large radiation belts around them as well.

Cumulative radiation dose causes a charge trapping in the oxide layers, which manifests as a parametric change in the devices. Total dose effects may be a function of the dose rate, and annealing of the device may occur, especially at elevated temperatures. Annealing refers to the self-healing of radiation induced defects. This can take minutes to months, and is not applicable for lattice damage. The internal memory or registers of the cpu are the most susceptible area of the chip, and are usually deactivated for operations in a radiation environment. The gross indication of radiation damage is the increased power consumption of the device, and one researcher reported a doubling of the power consumption at failure. In addition, failed devices would operate at a lower clock rate, leading to speculation that a key timing parameter was being effected in this case.

Single event upsets (seu's) are the response of the device to direct high energy isotropic flux, such as cosmic rays, or the secondary effects of high energy particles colliding with other matter (such as shielding). Large transient currents may result, causing changes in logic state (bit flips), unforeseen operation, device latch-up, or burnout. The transient currents can be monitored as an indicator of the onset of SEU problems. After SEU, the results on the operation of the processor are unpredictable. Mitigation of problems caused by SEU's involves self-test, memory scrubbing, and forced resets.

The LET (linear energy transfer) is a measure of the incoming particles' delivery of ionizing energy to the device. Latch-up refers to the inadvertent operation of a parasitic SCR (silicon control rectifier), triggered by ionizing radiation. In the area of latch-up, the chip can be made inherently hard due to use of the Epitaxial process for fabrication of the base layer. Even the use of an Epitaxial layer does not guarantee complete freedom from latch-up, however. The next step generally involves a silicon on insulator (SOI) or Silicon on Sapphire (SOS) approach, where the substrate is totally insulated, and latch-ups are not possible. This is an expensive approach,

In some cases, shielding is effective, because even a few millimeters of aluminum can stop electrons and protons. However, with highly energetic or massive particles (such as alpha particles, helium nuclei), shielding can be counter-productive. When the atoms in the shielding are hit by an energetic particle, a cascade of lower energy, lower mass particles results. These can cause as much or more damage than the original source particle.

Cumulative dose and single events

The more radiation that the equipment gets, in low does for a long time, or in high does for a shorter time, the greater the probability of damage.

These events are caused by high energy particles, usually protons, that disrupt and damage the semiconductor lattice. The effects can be upsets (bit changes) or latch-ups (bit stuck). The damage can "heal" itself, but its often permanent. Most of the problems are caused by energetic solar protons, although galactic cosmic rays are also an issue. Solar activity varies, but is now monitored by sentinel spacecraft, and periods of intensive solar radiation and particle flux can be predicted. Although the Sun is only 8 light minutes away from Earth, the energetic particles travel much slower than light, and we have several days warning. During periods of intense solar activity, Coronal Mass Ejection (CME) events can send massive streams of charged particles outward. These hit the Earth's magnetic field and create a bow wave. The Aurora Borealis or Northern Lights are one manifestation of incoming charged particles hitting the upper reaches of the ionosphere.

Cosmic rays, particles and electromagnetic radiation, are omni-directional, and come from extra-solar sources. Most of them, 85%, are protons, with gamma rays and x-rays thrown in the mix. Energy levels range to 10^6 to 10^8 electron volts (eV). These are mostly filtered out by Earth's atmosphere. There is no such mechanism on the Moon, where they reach and interact with the surface material. Solar flux energy's range to several Billion electron volts (Gev).

Other interesting problems plague advanced electronics off-planet. The Hughes (Boeing) HS 601 series of communications spacecraft suffered a series of failures in 1992-1995 due to failed relays. In zero gravity, tin "whiskers" grew within the units, causing them to short. The control processors on six spacecraft were effected, with three mission failures because both computers failed. This was highly noticeable, as the satellites were communication relays for

41

television. The Whisker phenomenon is now well understood, and mitigated.

Mitigation Techniques

The effects of radiation on silicon circuits can be mitigated by redundancy, the use of specifically radiation hardened parts, Error Detection and Correction (EDAC) circuitry, and scrubbing techniques. Hardened chips are produced on special insulating substrates such as Sapphire. Bipolar technology chips can withstand radiation better than CMOS technology chips, at the cost of greatly increased power consumption. Shielding techniques are also applied.

EDAC can be done with hardware or software, but always carries a cost in time and complexity. A longer word than needed for the data item allows for the inclusion of error detecting and correcting codes. The simplest scheme is a parity bit, which can detect single bit (or an odd number of errors, but can't correct anything. EDAC is applied to memory and I/O, particularly the uplink and downlink.

The effects of radiation on silicon circuits can be mitigated by redundancy, the use of specifically radiation hardened parts, Error Detection and Correction (EDAC) circuitry, and scrubbing techniques. Hardened chips are produced on special insulating substrates such as Sapphire. Bipolar technology chips can withstand radiation better than CMOS technology chips, at the cost of greatly increased power consumption. Shielding techniques are also applied. In error detection and correction techniques, special encoding of the stored information provides a protection against flipped bits, at the cost of additional bits to store. Redundancy can also be applied at the device or box level, with the popular Triple Modular Redundancy (TMR) technique triplicating everything, and based on the assumption that the probability of a double failure is less than that of a single failure. Watchdog timers are used to reset systems unless they are themselves reset by the software. Of course, the watchdog timer circuitry is also susceptible to failure.

Thermal issues

Radiation is not the only problem. In space, things are either too hot or too cold. On the inner planets toward the Sun, things are too hot. On the planets outward of Earth, things are too cold. In space, there is no gravity, so there are no convection currents. Cooling is by conduction and radiation only. This requires heat-generating electronics to have a conductive path to a radiator. That makes board design for chips, and chip packaging, complex and expensive.

Parts can be damaged by excessive heat, both ambient and self-generated. In a condition known as *thermal runaway*, an uncontrolled positive feedback situation is created, where overheating causes the part to further overheat, and fail faster.

Power constrained

Once they leave the Earth, the systems are on their own as regards to power. Generally, solar power is used. Deep space missions, very far from the sun, may rely on nuclear power.

Remote debugging

Debugging remote systems in orbit and on the surface of other planets present unique challenges. One of these is the significant delay in the communications link over interplanetary distances. Systems should ideally be self-diagnosing, because the cost to "phone home" is high.

Mechanical issues

In zero gravity, every thing floats, whether you want it to or not. Floating conductive particles, bits of solder or bonding wire, can short out circuitry. This is mitigated by conformal coatings, but the perimeter of the integrated circuit die is usually maintained at ground potential, and cannot be coated due to the manufacturing sequence.

The challenges of electronics in space are daunting, but much is now understood about the failure mechanisms, and techniques to address them.

ESD sensitivity

Solid state devices are particularly susceptible to *electrostatic discharge* (ESD) effects. These effects can involve very large voltages that cause device breakdown. Certain semiconductor lattice structures that have been damaged can actually "heal" over time, a process called annealing. Passive parts are sensitive to ESD as well. As parts are made smaller, the susceptibility to ESD effects increases. Proper grounding helps with ESD, providing a consistent voltage across components, without significant differences. ESD can cause parametric changes, which shift the device out of its nominal tolerance region. Over time, parametric changes may go unnoticed as they build, and lead to sudden catastrophic failure.

Bad Parts

Another issue is substandard parts, manufactured with an eye to low price and increased sales. Some of these are reversed-engineered or pirated parts. They may bear the same markings and internal identification codes as the legitimate part, and are difficult to tell from the genuine article. This becomes a major problem in military and aerospace applications, although commercial systems are also vulnerable. Software is also subject to "knock-off" versions.

Besides a reliability issue, counterfeit parts cause security concerns in critical systems. A major player in the identification of counterfeit parts is the University of Maryland's Center for Advanced Life Cycle Engineering. It has found that a major source of problems is the large volume of "scrap" electronics sent overseas for recycling and disposal.

Programs such as the Trusted Integrated Circuit (TIC), aim to develop new approaches to test and ensure the integrity of such components.

A counterfeit highly complex chip is hard to detect. You could examine the chip die for full compliance with the design specification, but this is expensive. You could check the product ID on the chip, but this can certainly be faked.

A cheap knock-off chip can be marked properly, and pass functional tests, but fail early due to production issues. Malicious circuitry/code can be included, locked away and hidden from view. Depending on the requirements of the embedded device, get the paper trail and buy from a trusted supplier. Be aware of the problem.

Underwater

What are the problems in this domain? The obvious one – the system gets wet. If its salt water, the system corrodes. Water is not a great communications media, except for sound, and that's limited bandwidth. There are some selected light frequencies that can be used. Let's not forget pressure – the deeper you go, the more pressure the system is exposed to.

In Arctic regions, we have thermal issues, and drifting ice. Also, in the subfreezing temperatures, there is essentially no relative humidity, and arcing can occur. In the deep ocean, thermal vents pump out extremely hot, caustic water, under enough pressure that it doesn't boil.

The systems need to have onboard batteries, because solar panels won't receive enough sunlight to be of any use. A tether to the surface, for shallow systems can also provide power, as could a small RTG, such as used in space missions.

Deep sea or Sea floor mining takes place at depths of 1,400-3800 meters, near hydrothermal vents, and are a good source of valuable metals. The best current site is at 1,600 meters depth in the Bismarck Sea, near New Ireland, Papua New Guinea. ROV's are used to obtain samples. The prime location is near hydrothermal vents on the sea floor at depths of 1500 to 3500 meters. Mining at these depths is done because the vents bring up quantities of rare metals from deeper in the Earth's crust. This includes copper, nickel, manganese. and gold. For technology manufacturing, cobalt, vanadium, molybdenum, and platinum are also useful. The actual mining is done by hydraulic suction, or a continuous line bucket system.

In the volcano

The Robotics group at Carnegie-Mellon University is headed by the famed Red Whittaker, who lead the CMU team to win the DARPA Challenge. He is also heading the team focused on the Google Lunar X Prize. One of his many projects was a mobile platform, *Dante*, designed to enter an active volcano.

In December of 1992, Dante and his support team ventured to active Mount Erebus in Antarctica, 12,450 feet high, and about 800 miles from the pole. Erebus is important enough that manned attempts were made to enter the caldera, all unsuccessful. How much the volcano contributes to the hole in the ozone layer above Antarctica is not known. The ozone layer blocks ultraviolet light from the sun, and is critical to the continuance of life on Earth. The robot made the descent to the crater floor, some 850 feet from the top. Here it took temperature measurements, and gas samples. Erebus tends to erupt in a minor fashion several times a day. This was a NASA Project, supported by the National Science Foundation. The temperature proved to be around 1,100 degrees from the corrosive gases vented by the volcano.

Dante is a six-legged walking robot, weighing close to 1000 pounds, and connected to the support team outside the volcano by a tether to provide power and data, and possible retrieval if the robot becomes disabled.

In August of 1994, and upgraded version of the robot, Dante 2, explored the active Alaskan volcano, Mount Spurr. This is located some 80 miles west of Anchorage. The descent into the caldera was 650 feet. The robot was monitored from a control facility in Anchorage, via a satellite link, providing a live video feed.. Dante-2 was bulked up at 1,700 pounds, having been redesigned based on the Earlier robot's lessons-learned. It was able to explore underneath a rock ledge, that had blocked an aerial view of a part of the crater. After successfully completing its mission, the robot walked its way out of the crater.

CMU Rovers have also been used in mine mapping. A rover called Groundhog went into an abandoned Pennsylvania coal mine and sent out live video to a conference on Mine Safety in 2002. They primary usage for the robots is seen as mapping. After initial tests, the concept of a wheeled rover was reconsidered, and an amphibious robot will be designed. This is because old mines are frequently flooded.

Polar Regions

The Arctic and Antarctic environments present the coldest temperatures on Earth, as well as other challenges for systems. In the area of parts and components, there are readily available high temperature parts, but not as many rated for colder temperatures. In addition, the environment is very dry, leading to static electricity build-up. Uneven terrain, from non-linear freezing of the ice, and from wind blown drift is encountered. Adding to this is the possibility of deep crevasses, and near white-out conditions due to strong winds blowing snow.

Oil drilling and transport takes place in the Canadian arctic and Alaska, allowing for the possibility of major environmental issues. In addition, for half the year, the Sun is at or below the horizon, and magnetic compasses do not work near the poles.

Examples of Embedded Systems in Extreme Environments

There are many domains and case studies in this area, but we can only look at a selected few. Some of these stories do not have a happy ending.

Automotive Electronics

The modern automobile (circa 2015) is a moving network of 100's of computers. If one of them fails, you might not be able to get your window down, or you might accelerate into the big truck in front of you. You might not be able to turn on the radio, or you might find your brakes or steering doesn't work.

An automobile is a hostile environment, not so much in the passenger cabin, but in the engine compartment and underneath, on the greasy side.

Down the borehole

Wells are used to retrieve underground oil and gas, water, geothermal fluids, and more. In Iceland, wells provide hot, highly corrosive water for electrical generation. What the drillers send down the bore hole other than the drill bit is highly technical.

They measure temperature, and do acoustic imaging of the walls and cutting face. As you bore into the Earth, the temperature increases about 25-30 degrees C per kilometer. More if you drill into a seismic active or volcanic zone. In a fracture zone, molten rock might be just under the surface. Today's drilling technology allows gas wells to ten kilometers, where the temperatures are 250 degrees C.

If you don't get it right, you get an incident like the 2010 BP blowout in the Gulf of Mexico.

So, you have these sensors down near the drill head, which is rotating. How do you get you data up to the surface. Radio isn't going to work. Data is taken when the drill is operating, with a measurement while drilling (MWD) enabled tool. Data is sent to the surface by modulating the mud (no kidding). This is at acoustic frequencies, so the data rate is low, less than 10 bps. But it works.

High temperature sensors are needed for monitoring bore hole temperature, pressure, and flow. In addition, there is the vibration and generated heat from the drilling operation going on.

In an operating well, after the boring (part) is finished, you still need to monitor these parameters. Another potential hazardous material encounter is free hydrogen at high temperatures. This can cause embrittlement of metals. The industry is going in the direction of smart wells, with more sensors and computing power down the hole.

NASA Rovers in Antarctica

NASA sponsored the Robotics Institute at Carnegie Mellon University to build the Nomad Rover, a 4-wheeled, 1,600 pound autonomous explorer. It was deployed in Antarctica in the year 2000. It's job is to find meteorites. It turns out, a lot of the meteorites found in Antarctica are from Mars, based on chemical composition. Nomad is doing the a similar job on Earth to what the Mars Rovers are doing on Mars.

Nomad is equipped with a laser rangefinder, high resolution cameras, onboard computer, satellite data link, and a gasoline-powered generator. It is looking for meteorites on the ice with a specific set of characteristics. If one is detected, it navigates to the target for a closer look. It has an arm with a camera and spectrometer, as well as a metal detector. If the rock meets the profile of being a potential meteorite, the GPS location is logged. The robot does not collect samples, but does sort through rock fields for items of interest. A rock the size of a potato (Allan Hills 84001) found in Antarctica in 1984 definitely came from Mars, and had chemical and fossil evidence of life. It is yet to be proven whether this definitely shows the past presence of life on Mars.

Greenland Rover (Grover)

This project is one in which the author had direct, hands-on experience. This was a project conducted over several summers at NASA/GSFC, by student interns. The concept was to have an autonomous vehicle collect data from an ice-penetrating radar units over large areas. The instrument was developed under an NSF Grant, and had been operated by two persons on skis, or by one person on a snowmobile. The Grover project was derived from a series of tracked sensor packages deployed in Antarctica, and conducted by a international team of 40 graduate and undergraduate students over several summers. The Program, sponsored by the GSFC Office of Education, was termed the Summer Robotics Boot Camp. The 40 students were selected from hundreds of applicants, and lead by a series of Mentors, chosen from NASA Civil Service and Contractor personnel.

The idea of the mission was to use an autonomous vehicle to collect data on the thickness of the Greenland ice sheet. Greenland, the largest island on the planet, has over 80% of its surface covered I ice. It is an autonomous country, under the Kingdom of Denmark. The ice towers to over 3200 meters above sea level. Temperatures reach down to -40 C. Because of the lack of trees, winds rush down form the polar regions, with no impediments to slow them.

There are two key questions about Greenland. One, how thick is the ice (with an associated question, is there land under it), and how fast is it melting. We know its melting, but we don't have the hard numbers. Significant melting of the Greenland ice pack could have severe impact on global sea levels, and overall temperatures.

The original Antarctic Rovers were small commercial tracked vehicles. The Grover was an extension to this, using a custom built aluminum chassis. It was powered by electric motors, supplied by lead acid batteries. Other battery technologies were too expensive. Waste heat from the computers was used to keep the batteries warm. The batteries were charged by large solar panels, but due to the low sun elevation at high latitudes, a hybrid wind turbine systems was added. Winds off the polar ice cap had essentially no obstruction before reaching lower latitudes, and blow continuously down the ice sheet.

The primary computational resource was a pc-class dual-core Intel ATOM-based motherboard. This interfaced to the instrument, formatted, and stored the data in a solid state drive. The volume of data collect was about 4-6 gigabytes per day, and the system was sized for 3 months of autonomous operation. Communication with the autonomous vehicle was via Iridium satellite modem, with text messages. This was adequate for command uplink, and status message downlink. For testing, the Grover included wifi for a local area network mobile connection.

The Grover unit had a GPS for location, encoders on each motor to track distance traveled, obstacle avoidance sensors, a compass sensor, battery and motor current and voltage sensors, sun sensors, and distributed temperature sensors.

The main computer ran an application in the Python language, and various distributed embedded controllers based on the Arduino architecture were used. There was a watchdog computer for computer problems, temperature, and anomalies. A reset could be commanded over the Iridium link.

The unit could be controlled directly with a wired pendant for testing, and through the wifi or Iridium link. It could also operated in autonomous mode, following predefined patterns.

During filed tests of the unit at NASA's Wallops Flight Facility in 2011, a quadcopter unit was used to make a video of the vehicle's performance from a "god's eye" view. It was later realized this capability could be used operationally, with the rover and the copter operating cooperatively. The rover would provide a landing spot and battery recharging station for the copter, and the copter could scout ahead of the rover for ice fissures, and areas of potential interest. This would provide a level of cooperation between the two systems.

Performance in field tests is seen in the excerpt from the Test summary:

"The motors routinely produced enough power and torque to move the robot at max speed (1.2 mph) in all terrain conditions (wet sand, hard packed sand, and soft dry sand). The Solar Arrays are about 13% efficient. In partly cloudy conditions with Sun almost overhead, the sunlit panels produced an average 216 W (with both panels). The other side produced an average 65 W, from non-direct sunlight and from sunlight reflected off the ocean and sand. The average wind Speed was 13 mph, which is typical of what we anticipate for the Greenland Ice Summit. This produced an average of 78 W from two wind turbines There was absolutely no indication of any tipping of the vehicle even in 40 mph gusts, which we have also experienced with it previously. The vehicle is very stable and durable and it has enough torque as currently geared, to drag a 225lb load through the sand behind it with an additional 100W of power. The load for this chassis design without the Instrument was 360W in the Driving mode and 50W in Idle mode. We anticipate another 100W worst case for the Instrument operational mode.

The tests performed on the power systems prove that GROVER will have over a 30% duty cycle in nominal Greenland Summit conditions, for the fully loaded Instrument operational mode. We are now designing a lighter version of the vehicle with more efficient solar arrays and batteries, which we expect to be 200lbs lighter and will take 100W less power to operate. Our goal then is to get above 50% operational duty cycle for nominal conditions. Note that on the beach under conditions of 10mph wind and clear sunshine, we were power positive, so we have justification for confidence that we can achieve a minimum of 50% duty cycle in nominal Greenland conditions. This is akin to operating in the daytime only around here. Also, we can easily adjust the gear ratios to drive the vehicle faster if desired."

Reference:
http://www.nasa.gov/topics/earth/features/grover.html#.U5G2T3af blc

I encouraged the cadre of eager engineering students to prevent failure modes in the system by saying that if the system failed in the field, they would be dropped next to it with a screwdriver and a voltmeter, and could ride it back to the base when it was fixed.

UAV's, or unmanned aerial vehicles, have applications in exploration. They have been used by the oil and gas industry to survey large areas for potential new resources. This generally involves geomagnetic sensing, looking for anomalies in the Earth's magnetic field which can be associated with underground cavities. In addition, drones with real-time video feeds can patrol long pipelines through remote areas looking for leaks. Similar uses can be found in the Electric Power Industry, for inspection of power lines in remote regions. There are manufacturers of commercial drones for commercial and scientific use. NASA operates an unarmed version of the General Atomics MQ-9 Reaper as part of its Environmental Research Aircraft and Sensor Technology (ERAST) Program. This program uses the aircraft for remote environmental sensing, monitoring of agriculture, severe storm tracking, and also serving as a telecomm relay platform.

Lorax – Life on Ice

Lorax is a project of CMU's Robotics Institute, and the name stands for Life on Ice: Robotic Antarctic Explorer. This is an autonomous system to survey the population of microbes on the Antarctic ice sheet. Such extremophiles are known to exist on Earth. A team from Colorado University in Boulder found microbes thriving on the high slopes of Andean volcanoes, surviving heat, ultraviolet radiation, and noxious gases. Bacteria are often seen in the soil after a glacier retreats. These environments are not much different than those on Mars. This is a NASA sponsored project.

One goal of this project is autonomous operation for a month. It uses both solar power and wind power. A model was tested in 2005 on a frozen lake bed in New Hampshire. It successfully traversed 14 kilometers autonomously, and returned to its starting point. It is a 4-wheeled vehicle.

Nereid-under-Ice

In the Arctic, a tele-presence The ROV is named Nereid Under-Ice, and was developed at Woods Hole Oceanographic Institution. It includes high definition video, a manipulator arm, and a large sensor suite. It completed its first expedition in 2014. It travels up to 40 km from the mother-ship, and is rated to a depth of 2,000 meters. It uses a lithium-ion battery pack. It does both acoustic and optical imaging. All of the sensed data is stored on board, and delivered in real time to the surface. A Fiber optic tether for communications is used, implementing gigabyte Ethernet. There is the distinct possibility that remote operation of the ROV from anywhere on the planet can be implemented, so guest scientists can remain at their home institutions (cozy and warm).

Exploring our Solar System

This section discusses the flight computers for missions to the other planets of our solar system. Each represents unique challenges. Earth's moon is the only extraterrestrial body to be visited by Man (so far). The amount of diversity among the planets, their associated moons, comets, asteroids, and other strange items is staggering.

We have had a closer look at most other bodies in our solar system, mostly by fly-by's, but have landed rovers on several. Probes have gone to examine 13 minor planets, asteroids or dwarf planets as well.

Exploring the Moon

The Moon was the first extra-terrestrial body to be explored. It is close enough that the communication time is about ½ second, and lunar spacecraft could be controlled from Earth. But, the lack of communication with the craft when they are behind the moon, from the Earth viewpoint, dictated at least a stored command capability. Rovers on the face of the moon towards Earth are in continuous contact.

Early in the era of space exploration, a series of rover vehicles were sent to the Earth's moon. These were designed as precursors to a manned visit. From the mid-1960's through 1976, there were some 65 unmanned landings on the moon. Now, this is the subject of a private effort, the Google X-prize. The moon is still the subject of intense study, with missions from the United States, Russia, China, India, the European Union, and Japan.

The Soviet Union launched a series of successful lunar landers, sample return missions, and lunar rovers. The Lunokhod missions, from 1969 through 1977, put a series of remotely controlled vehicles on the lunar surface.

The NASA Surveyor missions of 1966-68 landed seven spacecraft on the surface of the moon, as preparation for the Apollo manned missions. Five of these were soft landings, as intended. All of these were fixed instrument platforms.

Yutu is the name of the Chinese Lunar Rover, and means Jade Rabbit. It was launched in December of 2013. It landed successfully on the moon, but became stationary after the second lunar night. It is a 300 pound vehicle with a selection of science instruments, including an infrared spectrometer, 4 mast-mounted cameras including a video camera, and an alpha particle x-ray spectrometer. The rover is equipped with an arm. It also carries a ground penetrating radar. It is designed to enter hibernation mode during the 2-week lunar night. It does post status updates to the Internet, and still serves as a stationary sensor platform.

The latest mission to study the Moon is the Lunar Reconnaissance Orbiter, LRO, from NASA/GSFC. It was launched in 2009, and is still operating. It is is a polar orbit, coming as close as 19 miles to the lunar surface. It is collecting the data to construct a highly detailed 3-D map of the surface. Up to 450 Gigabits of data per day are returned to Goddard.

The LRO uses the RAD750 processor, on a CompactPCI 6U circuit card. The card provides a 1553 bus interface, and a 4-port Spacewire router. The cpu has 36 Megabytes of rad-hard sram, 4 megabytes of EEProm, and a 64k ROM. The SpaceWire functionality is provided by an ASIC chip, with access to its own 8 megabytes of SRAM. The transport layer of the Spacewire protocol is implemented in the ASIC in hardware. The 1553 interface is implemented in an FPGA

The cpu operates with a 132 MHz clock, and the backplane bus runs at 66 MHz. It consumes between 5 and 19 watts of power, and weighs around 3.5 pounds.

The cpu communicates to other spacecraft electronics over the backplane cPCI bus, the 1553, or the Spacewire. The High data volume camera uses the SpaceWire interface at up to 280 MHz, and other instruments use the 1553. The onboard data storage for data is a 400 gigabit mass memory unit, using SDRAM.

One interesting feature on the moon is the lava tubes, long channels left after lava flow. They exist on the Earth as well, and Mars. these might be exploited as lunar habitats, or shelters in case of radiation storms.

This section will discuss some of the other objects in our solar system, and how they have been explored, with discussions of the environments.

Exploring the Sun

We get all our energy from the huge thermal reactor some 8 light-minutes away. As you get closer to the Sun, its get hotter, and there is more radiation in terms of energetic particles.

NASA sent a series of probes to observe the sun in 1958 and for tens years after. These were the Pioneer 5-9 spacecraft. They didn't get any closer, but provided a different point of view. They got good data on the solar wind and the sun's magnetic field. Pioneer 9 sent back good data for 15 years. The Helios spacecraft in the 1970's were joint U.S.-German missions that used an orbit that got within the orbit of Mercury.

The 1980 Solar Maximum Mission observed the Sun in the spectrum of gamma rays, X-rays, and Ultraviolet. SMM had a failure in its electronics months after launch, but was repaired by a subsequent Shuttle mission. SMM used the NASA Standard Spacecraft Computer (NSSC-1) constructed of discrete logic elements. The author had flight software onboard SMM, when it reentered the atmosphere and burned in 1989.

A Japanese Mission to study the sun was Yohkoh, or Sunbeam, in 1991. It imaged solar flares in the x-ray spectrum.

Other US missions included SOHO, the Solar and Heliospheric Observatory, and the Solar dynamics Observatory. SOHO was located at the Lagrangian point between the Sun and the Earth, while is a null point in the gravity field. It sees the Sun constantly in many selected wavelengths.

The Solar Terrestrial Relations Observatory (Stereo) is a dual spacecraft mission to the Sun, launched in 2006. One is ahead of the Earth in orbit, the other behind. This gives three points of view of solar phenomena. Stereo's onboard computer uses the dual redundant Integrated Electronics Module (IEM) which has a RAD6000 cpu, as well as Actel FPGA's with soft-core P24 and CPU24 architectures. The P24 architecture is a 24-bit minimal instruction set computer (misc).

The Ulysses spacecraft, discussed later in the section on Jupiter, left the plane of the ecliptic (thanks to the Jupiter swing-by) and observed the Sun's high latitudes. One of its discoveries was that large magnetic waves emitted from the Sun scattered galactic cosmic rays.

The Genesis mission was designed to capture and return solar material. It achieved its goal, but was damaged in a crash landing when it returned to Earth in 2004.

Exploring Mercury

The U. S. Messenger mission to Mercury, the closest planet to the Sun, was launched in 2004. It is currently orbiting the hottest planet. It's Integrated Electronics Module has two Rad-Hard RAD6000 processors. One is the main, the other is a fault protection processor, operating at a slower clock rate (10 MHz vs 25 MHz). The modules are also duplicated. Two solid stage data recorders with 1 gigabyte of storage capacity each are used. No landing on Mercury has been attempted, although it would be feasible in the *twilight zone* between the extremely hot solar facing side, and the much colder space facing side. Mercury is in tidal lock with the sun, with one side always facing it. It wobbles a bit, creating a "twilight zone" that is mush less extreme.

Exploring Venus

The Soviet space program sent a series of probes to Venus. Early efforts were either crushed in the dense atmosphere, or suffered thermal damage. The Venera-7 mission had a goal of surface sample return. It struck the surface harder than planned, but returned temperature data for about 20 minutes. The Venera-8 probe returned data for some 50 minutes. Venera-13 and -14 returned color photos of the surface. Further Soviet and US efforts involved observation from Venus orbit. The Venus environment has proven extremely hostile. It seems our sister world, next towards the Sun from us, is in a environmental runaway condition. Heavy greenhouse clouds trap the solar energy, and cause massive global warming on a planetary scale. The surface temperature is high enough to melt some metals. This is very hard on computers, and electronics in general.

Venus' atmosphere is 96% carbon dioxide at a surface pressure of nearly 100 times Earth's, a greenhouse gone wild. It has no moons. Venus is roughly Earth-sized, but something went terribly wrong. It also has clouds of sulphuric acid, that landers have to get through. There is no magnetic field, but there is active volcanism.

Pioneer Venus observed Comet Halley while in transit. This was during a period when the comet was not visible from Earth, because of its proximity to the Sun. It monitored the loss of water from the comet as it swung around close to the Sun.

Venus express, an ESA mission, is in Venus Polar orbit. It found a massive double atmospheric vortex (storm) at the south pole.

Venus Express operated from 2005-2014.

Venus serves as a bad example of what environmnetal run-away can do to a planet the size of Earth.

Exploring the Asteroids

Asteroids have been imaged by the New Horizons spacecraft, on its way to Pluto, and by the Cassini spacecraft. The Pioneer-10 spacecraft was sent to study the far reaches of the solar system It passed through the Asteroid belt on its way to Jupiter and Saturn. It used a custom design, TTL discrete logic computer in 1972.

There are only 8 ½ planets, but there are thousands of asteroids, and it seems there may be as many types. This means that exploring the known asteroids is a daunting challenge. On the other hand, the asteroids can be a significant source of raw materials for Earth. But, a conventional survey and exploration approach would take too long. What is needed instead is a multitude of autonomous and flexible nano-spacecraft. The architectural model is a swarm (social insect model) distributed intelligence. The platform of low cost, low power, low weight could involve a nano-spacecraft with solar sails. The computation power of the individual nano-spacecraft can be combined into a "cluster of convenience" to address computationally challenging problems as they emerge, and on the spot.

Exploring Comets

The Deep Impact mission returned images of the surface of comet Borrelly in 2001. That surface was hot (26-70C), dry, and dark. In July of 2005, the same mission sent a probe into Comet Tempel 1. It created a crater, allowing imaging of subsurface material. Water ice was seen. Comet Borrely has a coma, which proved to be vaporized subsurface water ice. Deep Impact went on to complete a flyby of Comet Hartley-2 in 2010. The impactor used a RAD-750 flight computer with an imaging sensor, an inertial measurement unit, and four thrusters. It also included a star tracker, and an S-band communications link.

The 1999 Stardust mission retrieved sample material from the tail of Comet Wild 2 and returned it to Earth in 2006. The spacecraft computer was a RAD6000 with 128 megabytes of memory. The flight software took up 20% of the memory space, allowing for storing data when not in contact with Earth. The real time operating system was VxWorks. The comet material was captured in aerogel. Subsequently, 7 particles of interstellar dust were found in the aerogel. The mission also imaged the asteroids Annefrank, and was redirected to Tempel1 after the primary mission was complete. The RAD6000 cpu was used in the Command & Data Handling subsystem of Stardust.

ESA's Rosetta probe is in orbit around the comet Churyumov-Gerasimenko. It released a lander, Philae, which successfully touched down on the comet's surface in 2014. The onboard system has 3 gigabytes of solid state memory. The lander used a Harris RTX2020 processor. The lander communicated with the main spacecraft over a 32kbps link. It uses dual Mbyte, RAM, and EEPROM memory.

The memory size for the main processor was 1MWord RAM and 512 KWords EEPROM for each of 4 processors, and 512KWords PROM (redundant) accessible from each processor.

Exploring Mars

The Viking program was a pair of spacecraft sent to Mars in 1975. Each spacecraft consisted of an orbiter, and a lander. The Viking landers used a Guidance, Control and Sequencing Computer (GCSC) consisting of two Honeywell HDC 402 24-bit computers with 18K of plated-wire memory, while the Viking orbiters used a Command Computer Subsystem (CCS) with two custom-designed 18-bit bit-serial processors. There were 6 bits for the opcode, and 12 bits for the data address. The data format was 2's complement. The machine supported 32 interrupts. It was programmed in assembly language. The Honeywell machine had 47 instructions, and used two's complement representation for data. The architecture may have been derived from the Honeywell 316/516 models.

The Mars Pathfinder mission landed on Mars on July 4, 1997. It carried a Rover named Sojourner, which was a 6-wheeled design, with a solar panel for power, but the batteries were not rechargeable. The rest of the lander served as a base station. Communication with the rover was lost in September. The Rover used a single Intel 80C85 8-bit CPU with a 2 MHz clock, 64k of ram, 16 k of PROM, 176k of non-volatile storage, and 512 kbytes of temporary data storage. It communicated with Earth via the base station using a 9600 baud UHF radio modem. The communication loss leading to end of mission was in the base station communication, while the Rover itself remained functional. The Rover had three cameras, and an x-ray spectrometer.

The computer in the mission base station on Mars was a single RS-6000 CPU, with 1553 and VMEbuses. The software was the VxWorks operating system, with application code in the c language. The base station computer experienced a series of resets on the Martian surface, which lead to an interesting remote debugging scenario.

The operating system implemented pre-emptive priority thread (of execution) scheduling. The watchdog timer caught the failure of a task to run to completion, and caused the reset. This was a sequence of tasks not exercised during testing. The problem was debugged from Earth, and a correction uploaded.

The cause was identified as a failure of one task to complete its execution before the other task started. The reaction to this was to reset the computer. This reset reinitialized all of the hardware and software. It also terminates the execution of the current ground commanded activities.

The failure turned out to be a case of priority inversion. The higher priority task was blocked by a much lower priority task that was holding a shared resource. The lower priority task had acquired

61

this resource and then been preempted by several medium priority tasks. When the higher priority task was activated, it detected that the lower priority task had not completed its execution. The resource that caused this problem was a mutual exclusion semaphore used to control access to the list of file descriptors that the select() mechanism was to wait on.

The Select mechanism creates a mutex (mutual exclusion mechanism) to protect the "wait list" of file descriptors for certain devices. The vxWorks pipe() mechanism is such a device and the Interprocess Communications Mechanism (IPC) used was based on using pipes. The lower priority task had called Select, which called other tasks that were in the process of setting the mutex semaphore. The lower priority task was preempted and the operation was never completed. Several medium priority tasks ran until the higher priority task was activated. The low priority task attempted to send the newest high priority data via the IPC mechanism which called a write routine. The write routine blocked, taking control of the mutex semaphore. More of the medium priority tasks ran, still not allowing the high priority task to run, until the low priority task was awakened. At that point, the scheduling task determined that the low priority task had not completed its cycle (a hard deadline in the system) and declared the error that initiated the reset. The reset had the effect of wiping out most of the data that could show what was going on. This behavior was not seen during testing. It was successfully debugged and corrected remotely by the JPL team.

References
http://www.nasa.gov/mission_pages/mars-pathfinder/
http://research.microsoft.com/en-us/um/people/mbj/Mars_Pathfinder/

MER – Mars Exploration Rovers *Spirit & Opportunity*

The MER are six-wheeled, 400 pound solar-powered robots, launched in 2003 as part of NASA's ongoing Mars Exploration

Program. *Opportunity* (MER-B) landed successfully at Meridiani Planum on Mars on January 25, 2004, three weeks after its twin *Spirit* (MER-A) had landed on the other side of the planet. Both used parachutes, a retro-rocket, and a large airbag to land successfully, after transitioning the thin atmosphere of Mars.

For power, they use 140 watt solar arrays and Li-ion batteries. The Rovers require 100 watts for driving, One problem that was noted was that the Martian dust storms cover the solar panels with fine dust, reducing their efficiency. This resulted in the use of a radioisotope generator on a subsequent mission. It's been observed that Rovers often use more energy in path planning, than to execute the actual path.

The onboard computer uses a 20 MHz RAD6000 CPU with 128 MB of DRAM, 3 MB of EEPROM, and 256 MB of flash memory on a VME bus. There is a 3-axis inertial measurement unit, and nine cameras The Rovers communicate with Earth via a relay satellite in Mars orbit, the Mars Global Surveyor spacecraft. They also have the ability to communicate directly, at a lower data rate. The Spirit unit became stuck in 2009, and engineers were unable to free it after 9 months of trying. It was re-tasked as a stationary sensor platform. Contact was lost in 2010.

This is an ongoing mission. It was originally planned for 90 days, but the *Opportunity* Rover is still collecting useful data regarding potential life on our sister planet some 12 years later as of this writing. It has traveled over 35 kilometers on the Martian surface. Ground based test units are used at JPL for evaluating problems seen on Mars, and for evaluating software and procedural fixes.

The Mars Science Laboratory landed successfully on the Martian surface on August 6, 2012. It had been launched on November 26, 2011. It's location on Mars is the Gale crater, and was a project of NASA's Jet Propulsion Laboratory. It is designed to operate for two Martian years (sols). The mission is primarily to determine if Mars could have supported life in the past, which is linked to the presence of liquid water.

The Rover vehicle *Curiosity* weights just about 1 ton (2,000 lbs.) and is 10 feet long. It has autonomous navigation, and is expected to cover about 12 miles over the life of the mission. The platform uses six wheels The Rover Compute Elements are based on the BAE Systems' RAD-750 CPU, rated at 400 mips. Each computer has 256k of EEprom, 256 Mbytes of DRAM, and 2 Gbytes of flash memory. The power source for the rover is a radioisotope thermal power system providing both electricity and heat. It is rated at 125 electrical watts, and 2,000 thermal watts, at the beginning of the mission. The operating system is WindRiver's VxWorks real-time operating system.

The computers interface with an inertial measurement unit (IMU) to provide navigation updates. The computers also monitor and control the system temperature. All of the instrument control, camera systems, and driving operations are under control of the onboard computers.

Communication with Earth uses a direct X-band link, and a UHF link to a relay spacecraft in Mars orbit. At landing, the one-way communications time to Earth was 13 minutes, 46 seconds. This varies considerably, with the relative positions of Earth and Mars in their orbits around the Sun. At certain times, when they are on opposite sides of the Sun, communication is impossible.

The science payload includes a series of cameras, including one on a robotic arm, a laser-induced laser spectroscopy instrument, an X-ray spectrometer, and x-ray diffraction/fluorescence instrument, a mass spectrometer, a gas chromotograph, and a laser spectrometer. In addition, the rover hosts a weather station, and radiation detectors. There is cooperation between in-space assets and ground rovers in sighting dust storms by the meteorological satellite in Mars orbit.

References

http://www.nasa.gov/mars

www.nasa.gov/msl/

http://en.wikipedia.org/wiki/Mars_Science_Laboratory

www.space.com/16385-curiosity-rover-mars-science-laboratory.html

http://www.windriver.com/announces/curiosity/Wind-River_NASA_0812.pdf

Maven

NASA's Maven mission to Mars is an orbiter, to study the Martian atmosphere It was launched in November 2013, and reached Mars in September of 2014.

MAVEN is equipped with a RAD-750 Central Processing Board manufactured by BAE Systems in Manassas, Va. The processor can endure radiation doses that are a million times more extreme than what is considered fatal to humans. The RAD750 CPU itself can tolerate 200,000 to 1,000,000 rads. Also, RAD750 will not suffer more than one event requiring interventions from Earth over a 15-year period.

The RAD-750 was released in 2001 and made its first launch in 2005 aboard the Deep Impact Spacecraft. The CPU has 10.4 million transistors. The RAD750 processors operate at up to 200 megahertz, processing at 400 MIPS. The CPU has an L1 cache memory of 2 x 32KB (instruction + data) - to improve performance, multiple 1MB L2 cache modules can be implemented depending on mission requirements.

Mars Climate Orbiter

The spacecraft was lost on Mars in September 1999. The requirements did not specify units, so JPL used SI (metric) units and the contractor Lockheed Martin used English units. This was not caught in the review process, and led to the loss of the $125 million mission. The spacecraft crashed due to a navigation error.

The primary cause of this discrepancy was human error. Specifically, the flight system software on the Mars Climate Orbiter was written to calculate thruster performance using the metric unit Newtons (N), while the ground crew was entering course correction and thruster data using the Imperial measure Pound-force (lbf). This error has since been known as the *metric mix-up* and has been carefully avoided in all missions since by NASA.

"The root cause of the loss of the spacecraft was the failed translation of English units into metric units in a segment of ground-based, navigation-related mission software, as NASA has previously announced," said Arthur Stephenson, chairman of the Mars Climate Orbiter Mission Failure Investigation Board. "The failure review board has identified other significant factors that allowed this error to be born, and then let it linger and propagate to the point where it resulted in a major error in our understanding of the spacecraft's path as it approached Mars."

Reference   http://mars.jpl.nasa.gov/msp98/orbiter/

Mars Rover Pathfinder

The computer in the Mars Rover Pathfinder suffered a series of resets while on the Martian surface. The cpu Architecture was a single RS-6000 cpu, with 1553 and VMEbuses. The Software was the VxWorks operating system, with application code in c. Sensors and Actuators included Sun sensors, a star tracker, a radar altimeter, accelerometers, and the wheel drive.

The Root Cause was Priority Inversion in the operating system. Pre-emptive priority thread scheduling was used. The watchdog timer caught the failure of a task to run to completion, and caused the reset. This was a sequence of tasks not exercised during testing. The problem was debugged from Earth, and a correction uploaded.

The failure was identified by the spacecraft as a failure of one task to complete its execution before the other task started. The reaction to this by the spacecraft was to reset the computer. This reset reinitializes all of the hardware and software. It also terminates the execution of the current ground commanded activities.

The failure turned out to be a case of priority inversion (how this was discovered and corrected is a fascinating story – see refs.) The higher priority task was blocked by the much lower priority task that was holding a shared resource. The lower priority task had acquired this resource and then been preempted by several of the medium priority tasks. When the higher priority task was activated, to setup the transactions for the next databus cycle, it detected that the lower priority task had not completed its execution. The resource that caused this problem was a mutual exclusion semaphore used to control access to the list of file descriptors that the select() mechanism was to wait on.

The Select mechanism creates a mutex to protect the "wait list" of file descriptors for those devices which support select. The vxWorks pipe() mechanism is such a device and the IPC mechanism used is based on using pipes. The lower priority task had called Select, which had called other tasks, which were in the process of giving the mutex semaphore. The lower priority task was preempted and the operation was not completed. Several medium priority tasks ran until the higher priority task was activated. The low priority task attempted to send the newest high priority data via the IPC mechanism which called a write routine. The write routine blocked, taking control of the mutex semaphore.

More of the medium priority tasks ran, still not allowing the high priority task to run, until the low priority task was awakened. At that point, the scheduling task determined that the low priority task had not completed its cycle (a hard deadline in the system) and declared the error that initiated the reset.

References
http://www.nasa.gov/mission_pages/mars-pathfinder/
http://research.microsoft.com/en-us/um/people/mbj/Mars_Pathfinder/

Exploring the Gas Giants

The Gas giants are the planets Jupiter, Saturn, Uranus, and Neptune. These are the responsibility of the Jet Propulsion Laboratory. The RCA CMOS 1802 8-bit unit was used on JPL's Voyager, Viking and Galileo space probes. Prior to the Voyager mission, JPL was using simple sequencers purpose-built, and not based on a microprocessor architecture. This Command Computer System (CCS) architecture was 18-bit.

Pioneer 10 was the first mission to Jupiter, followed by Pioneer-11, and, as of this writing, there have been 8 total. Jupiter has a very high trapped radiation environment. There is also the interesting ring system, and Jupiter has 67 known moons. They are mostly all different, and some are thought to be capable of hosting life, as we know it. The moon Io has volcanic activity, and Europa has water ice on the surface.

The Voyager missions were originally terms the "Grand tour" and were to have visited Mars, Jupiter, and Saturn, with possibly some of the outer planets as well. The mission was called MJS-77. Budget constraints caused the mission to refocus on Jupiter and Saturn alone.

Voyager had a computer command subsystem (CCS) that controlled the imaging cameras. The CCS was based on an earlier design used for the Viking mission. The Attitude and Articulation control system (AACS) controlled the orientation of the spacecraft, and the movement of the camera platform. It is essentially the same computer as the CCS. The Data computer was constructed from a custom 4-bit CMOS component.

The ESA/NASA Ulysses mission visited the Jupiter system in 1992 and 2000, and collected data on the magnetosphere. This was a swing-by mission, as Ulysses was primarily to observe the Solar poles. Ulysses used a 280w RTG for power as it swung far from the Sun. Ulysses did not have a flight computer, but used a custom built Central Terminal Unit (CTU) and tape recorders for data storage. Each had a capacity of 45 megabits. The unit had an Attitude and Orbital Control System (AOCS), a purpose built unit, dual redundant, weighting 100 kilograms.

Cassini observed the planet from close-up in the year 2000, and studied the atmosphere. It used RTG's for power, and MIL-STD-1750A control computers.

Galileo entered Jupiter orbit in 1995, and returned data on the planet and the four Galilean moons until 2003. Three of the moons have thin atmospheres, and may have liquid water. The moon Ganymede has a magnetic field. Galileo was in the right place at the right time to see the comet Showmaker-Levy-9 enter the Jovian atmosphere, and launched an atmospheric probe. Galileo used six of the 8-bit RCA 1802 microprocessors, operating at 1.6 MHz. These units had been fabricated on a sapphire substrate for radiation hardness. The Attitude and Articulation Control System (AACS) used two bit-slice machines built from AMD2901 chips.

Saturn

Saturn has been visited by spacecraft four times. The first was a flyby by Pioneer-10 in 1979. This showed the temperature of the planet was 250 degrees K. Voyager-1 visited in 1980. It conducted a close flyby of the moon Titan to study its atmosphere. It is, unfortunately, opaque in visible light. Voyager-2 swung by a year later, and data showed changes in the rings since its sister mission the year before. Temperature and pressure profiles of the atmosphere were gathered. Saturn's temperature was measured at 70 degrees above absolute zero at the top of the clouds, and -130 c near the surface. The flybys discovered additional moons, and small gaps in the rings.

Cassini was the fourth spacecraft to study Saturn., which has rings, although smaller than Jupiter. The rings were confirmed by the Voyager spacecraft in the 1980's. Cassini entered into Saturnian orbit, and is still returning data. The one-way communications time varies form 68-84 minutes. It has also collected data on the Saturnian moons Titan, Enceladus, Mimas, Tethys, Dione, Rhea, Iapetus, and Helene. Things are strange in the Saturnian system. Cassini observed a hurricane in 2006 on the planet's south pole. It appears to be stationary, 5,000 miles across, 40 miles high, with winds of 350 mph. The large moon Titan has lakes of a liquid hydrocarbon, with possible seas of methane and ethane. Cassini launched a probe *Huygens* to Titan, and it landed on solid ground below the atmosphere. Huygenrs used a 1750A fight computer The Cassini mission was responsible for the discovery of seven new moons of Saturn.

Cassini observed the massive storm on Saturn, the great white spot, that recurs every 30 years. The storm, larger than the red one on Jupiter, exhibited a discharge that spiked the temperature 150 degrees. At the same time, Earth observations showed a large increase in atmospheric ethylene gas. It also discovered large lakes or seas of hydrocarbons near the planet's north pole.

Cassini discovered a possible atmosphere on the moon Enceladus, with ionized water vapor, and ice geysers. Many of the Saturnian moons are in tidal lock with their mother planet.

Uranus was imaged in a flyby by the Voyager-2 spacecraft in 1986. It also captures some images of the Uranian moon Umbriel.

Neptune has also been visited by Voyager-2 in 1989. It discovered six new moons, bringing the total to 14. That is the extent of close-up observations of the planet. Neptune has rings, like Jupiter and Saturn, and a great dark spot. It's moon Triton has geysers and polar caps. Triton has an interesting retrograde orbit – it goes in a different direction than the other moons. Triton's surface is mostly frozen nitrogen, and is geologically active. It is speculated that Triton has a subterranean ocean. The moon Ptoteus is an ellipsoid, not a sphere.

Exploring Pluto, and beyond

The New Horizons Mission spacecraft carries two computer systems, the Command and Data Handling system and the Guidance and Control processor. Each of the two systems is duplicated for redundancy, for a total of four computers. The processor used is the Mongoose-V, a 12 MHz radiation-hardened version of the MIPS R3000 CPU. Multiple clocks and timing routines are implemented in hardware and software to help prevent faults and downtime. There are dual redundant machines for the C&DH function, and two more for Attitude control.

To conserve heat and mass, spacecraft and instrument electronics are housed together in IEMs (Integrated Electronics Modules). There are two redundant IEMs. Including other functions such as instrument and radio electronics, each IEM contains computers.

In March of 2007, the Command and Data Handling computer experienced an uncorrectable memory error and rebooted itself, causing the spacecraft to go into safe mode. The craft fully recovered within two days, with some data loss on Jupiter's magnetotail.

In 2015, the Pluto flyby occurred, and data began to flow back to Earth. It took a year for all the imaging data to be transmitted, due to distances and transmit power involved.

Case studys, system failures in Harsh environments

This section discusses selected case studies of systems operating in extreme that went wrong..

Aerospace

Getting spacecraft off the surface of the planet and into orbit, or to other planets is somewhat difficult. There are many documented failure cases in this realm, not because the rocket scientists and engineers make more mistakes, but due to the difficulty of the environment. This is an area of particular interest to me, as I worked as a NASA support contractor since the 1970's on many missions. I have a lot of case studies in this area. A much more exhaustive study in the area is the book by Harland and Lorenz, dated 2005, which is in the reference section at the end of this book. There is a lot more material that happened since 2005, unfortunately.

Launch Vehicle Reliability

The first tricky part is getting the payload off the ground. This has been shown to be a hazardous task since the initial work by Von Braun in Germany, and Robert Goddard, in the U. S. Let's keep in mind that Robert Goddard was supposedly asked to stop his rocket launches by the Fire Marshall. If the launch vehicle fails, the payload is irrelevant. We'll look at a few launch vehicle failures.

The launch environment is harsh, with extremes of vibration, acoustics, and the possibility of exposure to toxic propellants and caustic liquids.

Titan Launch Vehicle

In 1999, a Titan IV-B with a Centaur upper stage and Milstar satellite left Cape Canaveral Air Station, bound for geosynchronous orbit. After the Centaur second stage with the payload separated from the Titan booster at 9 minutes into the flight, things started to go wrong. Instability in the roll axis became pitch and yaw axis instability which became uncontrolled tumbling. The Centaur struggled to control these errors, but depleted its available propellant. The Milstar payload ended up in the wrong orbit. The mission was declared a complete loss by the Secretary of the Air Force, with a cost of around a billion dollars. This was the third straight failure of a Titan mission, and got extensive interest from the Media.

The Accident Investigation Board reach the conclusion that the problem was due to a "failed software development, testing, and quality assurance process." Human error was the cause of an incorrect entry of a value for the roll rate filter constant. This was seen during testing, but not recognized as an error, the consequences were not appreciated, and the error was not corrected. The software development process was shown to allow single point failures. The Independent Verification and Validation (IV&V) Process was not applied to the roll rate filter constant.

Reference
sunnyday.mit.edu/accidents/titan_1999_rpt.doc
http://www.spacedaily.com/news/titan-99e.html
http://www.youtube.com/watch?v=ZFeZkrRE9wI

Ariane 5

The European Ariane 5 launch vehicle was a follow-on to, and improvement of the Ariane-4. These were launched from a site in French Guiana near the Equator, to take maximum advantage of the Earth's rotation. Ariane 5's first test flight (Flight 501) in June, 1996 failed, with the rocket self-destructing 37 seconds after launch because of a malfunction in the control software. A data conversion from 64-bit floating point value to 16-bit signed integer value to be stored in a variable representing horizontal bias caused a processor trap (operand error) because the floating point value was too large to be represented by a 16-bit signed integer. The software was originally written for the Ariane 4 where efficiency considerations (the computer running the software had an 80% maximum workload requirement) led to 4 variables being protected with a handler while 3 others, including the horizontal bias variable, were left unprotected because it was thought that they were "physically limited or that there was a large margin of error". The software, written in Ada, was included in the Ariane 5 through the reuse of an entire Ariane 4 subsystem despite the fact that the particular software containing the bug, which was just a part of the subsystem, was not required by the Ariane 5 because it has a different preparation sequence than the Ariane 4. The incident resulted in a loss of over $500 million. The launch vehicle and its payload were scattered across square kilometers of mangrove swamp.

The Root Cause was a flight control system failure. Not a hardware error, but a software error, more of a math error. A diagnostic code from failed (Inertial Reference System) IRS-2 was interpreted as data. IRS-1 had failed earlier. The diagnostic data was sent because of a software error. The software module was only supposed to be used for alignment, not during flight. The diagnostic code was considered as a 64-bit floating point number, and converted to a 16-bit signed integer, but the value was too large to fit in 16 bits. This caused the rocket nozzles to steer hard-over to the side, causing the vehicle to veer off course and crash.

References
De Dalmau, J. and Gigou J. "Ariane-5: Learning from flight 501 and Preparing for 502,
http://esapub.esrin.esa.it/bulletin/bullet89/dalma89.html

Lions, Prof, J. L. (Chairman) ARIANE 5 flight 501 Failure, Report by the Inquiry Board, 19 July 1996,
http://www.esrin.esa.it/tidc/htdocs/Press/Press96/ariane5rep.html

Jezequel, Jean-Marc and Meyer, Bertrand "Design by Contract: The Lessons of Ariane," IEEE computer, Jan. 1997, vol 30, n. 2, pp129-130.

"Inquiry Board Traces Ariane 5 Failure to Overflow Error," http://siam.org/siamnews/general/ariance.html

Baber, Robert L. "The Ariane 5 explosion as seen by a software engineer," http://www.cs.wits.ac.za/~bob/ariane5.htm

Others

The Apollo-13 mission, with its survival of the oxygen tank explosion, has been well covered in the media, and in a movie. A lot to be said about redundancy there, as well as improvisation. The Lunar lander computer was re-purposed to control the Apollo vehicle back to Earth.

Soyuz TMA-1 flight computer problem

The new guidance computer of the Russian Soyuz TMA-1 caused an off-course landing in its first use in 2003. This was a concern for the crew of the International Space Station, as the Soyuz TMA-2 was docked to the station as the crew return vehicle, and it had the same computer. The Soyuz is normally controlled to skim the atmosphere to reduce its velocity, using a deceleration of 5g's. The center of gravity of the craft is off center by design, and by rolling the capsule, the tilt, and thus the lift, can be controlled. As in the Apollo days, too steep, you burn up, and too shallow, you skip off the atmosphere and head for space.

The TMS-1 autopilot lost its references, and switched to backup. This simple mode uses a roll maneuver to even out the path, while resulting in a deceleration twice that of the nominal mode, and a very short landing site, compared to the nominal. In this case, the crew returned safely, and were spotted by a rescue team within two hours.

It could have been worse. In 1965, the crew of the Voskhod-2, which had accomplished the first spacewalk, the capsule landed some 386 kilometers off course, and the crew had to spend the night in their capsule, due to the danger of bears and wolves in the area. Welcome back to Earth, tasty morsels!

Initially, the Soyuz error was attributed to the American crewman pushing the backup mode activation button, but this was refuted by the crew, A software cause was sought. Software problems of potentially fatal effect had happened in 1988 (with the crew catching the error in time), and again in 1997, where two potentially catastrophic flaws were caught and mitigated by human intervention. One of these would have fired the reentry rockets in the wrong direction. The software has since been corrected. The Soyuz remains the main delivery and return vehicle for the mixed crew of the International Space Station.

Reference

Oberg, James "Software bug sent Soyuz off course," NBC News, MSNBC.com,

Phobos-Grunt

In November of 2010, the Russian Space Agency launched an ambitious mission to set a probe down on the small Martian moon Phobos, collect samples, and return them to Earth.

There was a failure of the spacecraft propulsion system that stranded the mission in Earth orbit. It re-entered the Earth's atmosphere in January 2011.

Various causes were postulated for the failure, including interference by U.S. Radar, cosmic ray induced upsets, programming errors, and counterfeit chips.

The final report from Roscosmos cited software errors, failure of chips in the electronics, possibly due to radiation damage, and the use of non-flight qualified electronics, with inadequate ground testing. Evidently, identical chips in two assemblies failed nearly simultaneously, so quickly that an error message was not generated. It was possible that the error was recoverable, as the spacecraft entered a safe mode with a proper sun orientation for maximum power. However, the design precluded the reset mode before the spacecraft left its parking orbit. This was major design oversight.

The identified chips that failed were 512k SRAM (static random access memory. The part numbers from the Russian report were checked by NASA's Jet Propulsion Lab, and were found to be among the most radiation susceptible chips they had ever seen. Bad choice. The chips could last in space a few days, and were barely acceptable for non-critical applications, The probably failure cause was single event latch-up, which is sometimes recoverable. In single event latch up, there is a single particle strike that latches up a transistor, preventing it from operating. Usually, if you turn it off and back on again, it will work. A lot of radiation damage to the underlying semiconductor lattice fixes itself after a while, a process called "annealing."

References
Klotz, Irene "Programming Error Doomed Russian Mars Probe," Discovery News, Feb. 7, 2012, news.discovery.com

de Carbonnel, Alissa "Russia races to salvage stranded Mars probe, " Reuters, 2011. www.reuters.com
Amos, Jonathan "Phobos-Grunt mars Probe loses its way just after launch," 9 Nov. 2011, BBC News, www.bbc.co.uk

Oberg, James "Did Bad memory chips Down Russia's Mars Probe?.," Feb 2012, IEEE Spectrum, IEEE.org.

Friedman, Louis D. "Phobos-Grunt Failure Report Released," 2/6/2012, www.planetary.org/blogs/guest-blogs/lou-friedman

Phobos fail: What really happened to Russia's Mars Probe, Jan 19,

2012, RT.com.

Transportation

This section discusses failures in earthly modes of transportation, aircraft, highway, and rail. The (U. S.) National Transportation Safety Board (NTSB) keeps extensive databases of aviation events at:

http://www.ntsb.gov/investigations/reports_aviation.html

from their Mission Statement, on their website: "The National Transportation Safety Board is an independent Federal agency charged by Congress with investigating every civil aviation accident the United States and significant accidents in other modes of transportation – railroad, highway, marine and pipeline. The NTSB determines the probable cause of the accidents and issues safety recommendations aimed at preventing future accidents."

One of the natural hazards in aviation is wind shear, which is a sharp gradient in wind speed over a short distance. It can be either horizontal or vertical. All passenger aircraft must have a wind shear detection system, after a series of fatalities through the 1980's. In the previous 20 years, there were 26 accidents, with over 600 deaths. Yet, air travel is perhaps the safest mode of transportation, on average.

Air France 447, and the Automation Paradox

Aircraft accidents get a lot of out attention. Air travel is safer than ever, but generates big headlines when something goes wrong. In June of 2009, Air France 447 left Rio de Janeiro heading to Paris. It was an Airbus A330. Unfortunately, it crashed into the Atlantic Ocean, killing all passengers and crew. The cause was completely unknown for quite a while, since the wreckage could not be located. Two years afterwards, the flight data recorders were located and retrieved from the ocean floor at 13,000 feet.

The official report on the accident said "that the aircraft crashed after temporary inconsistencies between the airspeed measurements, likely due to the aircraft's pitot tubes being obstructed by ice crystals, caused the autopilot to disconnect, after which the crew reacted incorrectly and ultimately led to an aerodynamic stall from which they did not recover. So we have two problems here. One, the pitot tubes clogged up, so airspeed could not be measured accurately, and the crew reacted inappropriately. There were 3 pitot tubes, and the problem with in-flight icing was known since the early days of aviation. Pitot tubes are heated to counter this problem. Why this triple redundancy did not work in this case is not known, although there does seem to be a common-cause error, which removed the redundancy.

The autopilot disengaged after a period of turbulence, and one of the flight deck crew took manual control. The engines auto-thrust control also disengaged, as designed. Evidently, at this time, the pitot tubes iced over, and an accurate measurement of airspeed was lost. In the mode the aircraft was in, stall warning was disengaged. Stall is when there is not enough airflow over the wings to generate lift, usually caused by low speed, or excessive angle of attack of the wind. The aircraft had a reported angle of attack of 35 degrees, way too much. The engines were operating a full power, with the aircraft nose angled up 35 degrees, upon impact with the ocean.

The aircraft had transmitted a series of automated messages , among them that there was a detected fault in the Air Data Inertial Reference Unit, that there was a disagreement among the three independent air data systems, and that there had been a fault in the flight management guidance system.
From the recovered recorders, it became clear that the pilots did not have a clear idea of the planes speed, due to inconsistent information. The final report mentioned, among other causes, that the flight crew "made inappropriate control inputs."

Part of the problem has been attributed to the Automation Paradox, where an automatic systems usually works so well without human input (such as the autopilot), the human operators are mostly kept out of the loop until something unexpected happens. Over-reliance on automated systems leads to complacency. At the same time, both the computer controls, and the pilots were without a valid speed indication.

References
http://www.bea.aero/docspa/2009/f-cp090601.en/pdf/f-cp090601.en.pdf

Jean-Pierre Otelli (2011). Erreurs de pilotage : Tome 5 (Pilot Error: Chapter 5). Altipresse. ISBN 979-10-90465-03-9.

Roger Rapoport (2011). The Rio/Paris Crash: Air France 447. Lexographic Press. ISBN 978-0-9847142-0-9.

Palmer, Bill (2013). Understanding Air France 447 (William Palmer. p. 218. ISBN 9780989785723.

X-15, pushing the limits

The X-15 Research Aircraft could fly to the boundary of Space in the 1950's, and became a training tool for Astronauts. They were carried to 45,000 feet under the wing of a B-52 aircraft, and dropped, after which their rocket engine would take them to 66 miles high. After the rocket engine burned all its fuel, the X-15 would return unpowered, and land on the dry lake beds at Edwards Air Force Base. After separation from the B-52, the flight took 10 minutes to reach altitude and land. Since it went above the atmosphere, the aircraft also included small maneuvering jets for control.

On the 191-st flight of an X-15, in November of 1967, something went terribly wrong for Air Force Major Mike Adams. The first problem was a large electrical arc from an exterior probe into the electrical system, after engine ignition. This evidently effected the flight control system. Less than a minute later, a second arc occurred. The aircraft became unresponsive to pilot inputs. At the peak of its climb, the aircraft was a a right angle to its flight path.

This works ok if there's not much air. The pilot radioed to the ground the the aircraft "seems squirrelly." As the aircraft descended into denser air, it went into a spin, but the aerodynamic and thruster controls were able to stop this. However, at this point the aircraft was in an inverted dive, with violent oscillations in all three axes. The aircraft broke apart at 63,000 feet.

Lessons learned from this unfortunate incident were used to improve the Apollo Lunar Lander flight control system. Major Adams was posthumously awarded Astronaut Wings.

Reference
NASA system Failure Case Study, march 2011, Vol. 5, Issue 3.

Wrap-up

As difficult as it is to get an embedded system working correctly on the test bench, extreme environments, some that we might encounter every day, make the job much more difficult. There are no shortcuts, it has to be done right the first time, it has to be safe, it has to degrade gracefully, and fail safe. Not easy.

Glossary

Aerostat – flight system deriving left from buoyancy.

Api – applications program interface

Arduino – small embedded systems architecture.

ASIC – application specific integrated circuit. Specific hardware.

Atmosat – platform operating at high altitude in the atmosphere, for extended periods.

Bar – metric measurement of pressure; normal sea level atmospheric pressure is one bar.

Bit – smallest unit of binary information. Two states.

Bluetooth – a short range radio standard for data.

BSD – Berkeley Systems Distribution (of Unix)

Byte – collection of 8 bits.

C – a programming language.

C&DH – command and data handling.

Cubesat – small satellite that can be developed by schools or individuals (standard)

CMU – Carnegie Mellon University.

Codec – coder/decoder

copyleft – license for open source software

Cpu – central processing unit.

Dalvik – the virtual machine in Android.

DARPA – Defense Advanced Research Projects Agency.

Dc – direct current

Drone – unmanned aerial vehicle.

DSP – digital signal processor

DSN – NASA's Deep Space Network

duty cycle – percentage of "ON" in an on-off cycle.

eeprom – electrically erasable programmable read-only memory. Mostly superseded by
flash.

Endolithic – organism living withing rock, like algae or lichen

ESA – European Space Agency.

Ethernet – a networking protocol; wired or wireless.

FPGA – field programmable gate array.

Gbytes - 10^9 bytes.

GHz - 10^9 hertz

Gpio – general purpose input output

GPS – global positioning system, series of navigation satellites.

Grover – Greenland Rover.

GSGC – Goddard Space Flight Center, chief NASA Center for Earth observation.

HDMI – High Definition Multimedia Interface

Hexcopter - a small aircraft with six small horizontal rotors, like a helicopter.

IDE – Integrated Development Environment (toolset)

IoT – Internet of Things.

Iridium – a satellite system for global communications.

Isa – instruction set architecture.

Java – a programming language.

Kbytes – 10^3 bytes.

Lidar – radar, using light. Same thing, different frequency.

Linux – open source operating system; unix-like

LioP – lithium polymer battery technology.

Lorax – Life on Ice Robotic Antarctic Explorer – CMU project.

Lunokhod – Russian lunar probe; translates as "moonwalker"

Malware – malicious software.

Mbytes – 10^6 bytes.

MEMS - microelectronic mechanical systems – producing mechanical systems such as gyros using microelectronics fabrication technology.

MER – Mars Exploration Rover.

MEV – million electron volts, a measure of energy.

Metadata – data about the data. Date, time, modified? Etc. microcontroller – microprocessor plus memory and I/O.

mips – millions of instructions per second.

MSL – Mars Science Lab.

Multicore – computer architecture with multiple processors on one chip.

Mutex – a mutual exclusion mechanism in hardware (traffic light) or software.

84

MWD – measurement while drilling

NASA – National Aeronautics and Space Administration.

NOAA – National Oceanographic Atmospheric Administration.

NSF – National Science Foundation.

Pc – personal computer

pH – numeric scale for acidity (less than 7) or alkalinity (7 to 14)

Perigee – point of closest approach to Earth in a satellite orbit.

PWM – pulse width modulation; used for dc motor speed control.

Python – programming language; large man-eating snake.

Quadcopter – a small aircraft with four small horizontal rotors, like
    a helicopter.

Rov – remotely operated vehicle.

RTG – Radioisotope Thermal Generator.

S-band – radio frequency, 2-4 GHz.

Sata – a serial disk interface standard.

SatCom – satellite communications.

Seu – single event upset in electronics, due to radiation.

SSR – solid state recorder

Thermophile – organizism that prefers extreme high temperatures.

Uart – universal asynchronous receiver transmitter.

UAS – unmanned aerial system.

UaV – unmanned aerial vehicle, or remotely piloted aircraft, or
    drone.

Unix – operating system from Bel Labs, written in the c language.

URL – uniform resource locater. Used as a reference to a resource
    on the Internet.

Usb – universal serial bus, a communications standard.

Vga – a video display standard.

VxWorks – a real time operating system from Windriver.

WiFi – short range radio-based networking.

References

Albus, J.S.; Lumia, R.; McCain, H. "Hierarchical Control of Intelligent Machines Applied to Space Station Telerobots, IEEE Transactions on Aerospace and Electronic Systems, Sept 1988, V 24 n 5 pp 535-541.

Antonelli, Gianluca *Underwater Robots, Springer; 3rd ed. 2014, ISBN- 3319028766.*

Albus, James S. *System Description and Design Architecture for Multiple Autonomous Undersea Vehicles,* University of California Libraries, January 1, 1988, ISBN-10: 1125517441.

Albus, James A. *Brains, Behavior and Robotics*, McGraw-Hill Inc., 1st Edition, December 1, 1981, ISBN-10: 0070009759.

Anas, Brittany, "Researchers to Fly Unmanned Planes over Greenland," July 16, 2008, Scripps News.

Bar-Cohen, Yoseph (ed), Zacny, Kris (ed) *Drilling in Extreme Environments: Penetration and Sampling on Earth and other Planets,* 1st edition, 2009) ISBN-3527408525.

Bräunl, Thomas *Embedded Robotics: Mobile Robot Design and Applications with Embedded Systems* Springer; 2nd ed., 2006, ISBN- 3540343180.

Castelvecchi, Davide "Invasion of the Drones: Unmanned Aircraft Take Off in Polar Exploration, March 2010, Scientific American.

CMU "A Robot for Volcano Exploration," www.robovolc.dees.unict.it Carnegie Mellon University, Field Robotics Center, www.frc.ri.cmu.edu

Cook, Gerald *Mobile Robots: Navigation, Control and Remote*

Sensing, Wiley-IEEE Press; 1st ed, 2011, ISBN-0470630213.

Cressler, John D. (Ed), H. Mantooth, Alan (Ed) *Extreme Environment Electronics,* 1st Edition, CRC Press; 1 edition, 2012, ISBN-1439874301.

Del Castillo, Linda et al *Extreme Environment Electronic Packaging for Venus and Mars Landed Missions,* JPL, https://solarsystem.nasa.gov/docs/7_8DELCASTILLO_paper.pdf

Denis Flandre (Ed), Alexei Nazarov (Ed), Peter L.F. Hemment (Ed) *Science and Technology of Semiconductor-On-Insulator Structures and Devices Operating in a Harsh Environment*: Proceedings, 26-30 April 2004 (Nato Science Series II:) Springer; 2005 edition, ISBN-1402030126.

Dudek, Gregory; Jenkin, Michael *Computational Principles of Mobile Robotics* Cambridge University Press; 2nd ed, 2010, ISBN-0521692121.

Enzmann, Robert Duncan "Unmanned Exploration of Planetary Surfaces," Annals of the New York Academy of Sciences, Volume 163, Second Conference on Planetology and Space Mission Planning, pp 387–395, September 1969.

Finckenor, Miria M., de Groh, Kim *Space Environmental Effects, A Researcher's Guide to International Space Station,* NASA ISS Program Office,

General Electric, *Embedded Computing Technologies for Unmanned Vehicles*, 2010, GE Intelligent Platforms, www.ge-ip.com

Geologic Surveys: Mineral Exploration at the Ends of the Earth, Mining-Technology.com, Nov. 2010.

Hobbs, Chris *Embedded Software Development for Safety Critical*

Systems, Auerbach Publications, 2015, ISBN-1498726704.

Hunter, G. W. *High Temperature Wireless Communication And Electronics For Harsh Environment Applications,* 2013 , NASA Technical Reports Server (NTRS), ISBN-10: 1289089655.

Iagnemma, Karl; Dubowsky, Steven Mobile Robots in Rough Terrain: Estimation, Motion Planning, and Control with Application to Planetary Rovers, Springer, ISBN-10: 3642060269.

Keys, Andrew S.; Watson, Michael D. *Radiation Hardened Electronics for Extreme Environments* NASA/MSFC Document ID: 20070018806, 2007.

Kolawa, Elizabeth; Chen, Yuan; Mojarradi, Mohammad M.; Weber, Carissa Tudryn; Hunter, Don J. "A Motor Drive Electronics Assembly for Mars Curiosity Rover: An Example of Assembly Qualification for Extreme Environments," Document ID: 20130013010, 2013, Report Number: NF1676L-16070.

Kolawa, Elizabeth (Chied author) et al *Extreme Environment Technologies for Future Space Missions,* 2007, JPL D-32832, vfm.jpl.nasa.gov/files/EE-Report_FINAL.pdf

Leary, Warren E. "Robot Named Dante To Explore Inferno Of Antarctic Volcano." New York Times. December 8. 1992.

Leary, Warren E. "Robot Completes Volcano Exploration," New York Times, August 3, 1994.

Leary, Warren E., "Robot Is Nearing Goal Inside Active Volcano," New York Times, August 2, 1994.

Leary, Warren E., "Hunt for Meteorites In Antarctica Enlists a Novel Recruit," New York Times, January 18, 2000.

Leary, Warren E. "Hardier Breed of Antarctic and Lunar

Explorers: Robots," New York Times, May 13, 1997.

Leveson, Nancy G. *System Safety and Computers, Addison-Wesley, 1995, ISBN: 0-201-11972-2.*

Martin, Michael, Wallner, Elke *Deserts of the Earth* Thames & Hudson,2004, ISBN- 0500511942.

McCluskey, F. Patrick, Podlesak, Thomas,Richard Grzybowski, Richard *High Temperature Electronics* (Electronic Packaging), 1st Edition, CRC Press , 1996, ISBN-0849396239 .

Middleton, Nick *Extremes: Surviving the World's Harshest Environments,* Thomas Dunne Books, 2015, ASIN-B00SRYGJIS.
Moore, Steven W.; Bohm, Harry; Jensen, Vicky *Underwater Robotics: Science, Design & Fabrication,* Marine Advanced Technology Edu; 1st ed, 2010, ISBN-0984173706.

Patterson, David A., Hennessy, John L. *Computer Organization and Design The Hardware/Software Interface, ARM Edition,* Morgan Kaufman, 2017, ISBN 978-0-12-801733-3.

Petersen, Edward *Single Event Effects in Aerospace,* 1st Edition, Wiley-IEEE Press, 2011 ISBN-0470767499.

Rice, Doyle, "Unmanned Research Robots Destined to Roam Ice Sheets," Nov. 24, 2008, USA Today.

Seto, Mae L. (Ed) *Marine Robot Autonomy,* Springer; 2013 edition, 2012, ISBN- 1461456584.

Truszkowski, Walt *Autonomous and Autonomic Systems: With Applications to NASA Intelligent Spacecraft Operations and Exploration Systems,* Springer; 1st Edition. edition, 2009, ISBN-1846282322.

Truszkowski, Walt; Clark, P. E.; Curtis, S.; Rilee, M. Marr, G. *ANTS: Exploring the Solar System with an Autonomous Nanotechnology Swarm.* J. Lunar and Planetary Science XXXIII (2002)

Usher, M. J. and Keating, D. A. *Sensors & Transducers: Characteristics, Application., Instrumentation & Interfacing* 1996, Scholium International; 2nd edition, ISBN 0333604873.

Wadoo, Sabiha; Kachroo, Pushkin *Autonomous Underwater Vehicles: Modeling, Control Design and Simulation,* CRC Press, 2010, ISBN-1439818312.

Wang, Anbo *Harsh Environment Sensors II* (Proceedings of SPIE) illustrated edition Society of Photo Optical; 1999, ISBN-0819434450.

Wijesundara, Muthu and Azevedo, Robert *Silicon Carbide Microsystems for Harsh Environments* Springer; 2011 edition, ISBN-1441971203

Resource

http://users.eecs.northwestern.edu/~jhu304/files/lowtemp.pdf

If you enjoyed this book, you might also be interested in some of these.

Stakem, Patrick H. *16-bit Microprocessors, History and Architecture*, 2013 PRRB Publishing, ISBN-1520210922.

Stakem, Patrick H. *4- and 8-bit Microprocessors, Architecture and History*, 2013, PRRB Publishing, ISBN-152021572X,

Stakem, Patrick H. *Apollo's Computers*, 2014, PRRB Publishing, ISBN-1520215800.

Stakem, Patrick H. *The Architecture and Applications of the ARM Microprocessors*, 2013, PRRB Publishing, ISBN-1520215843.

Stakem, Patrick H. *Earth Rovers: for Exploration and Environmental Monitoring*, 2014, PRRB Publishing, ISBN-152021586X.

Stakem, Patrick H. *Embedded Computer Systems, Volume 1, Introduction and Architecture*, 2013, PRRB Publishing, ISBN-1520215959.

Stakem, Patrick H. *The History of Spacecraft Computers from the V-2 to the Space Station*, 2013, PRRB Publishing, ISBN-1520216181.

Stakem, Patrick H. *Floating Point Computation*, 2013, PRRB Publishing, ISBN-152021619X.

Stakem, Patrick H. *Architecture of Massively Parallel Microprocessor Systems*, 2011, PRRB Publishing, ISBN-1520250061.

Stakem, Patrick H. *Multicore Computer Architecture*, 2014, PRRB

Publishing, ISBN-1520241372.

Stakem, Patrick H. *Personal Robots*, 2014, PRRB Publishing, ISBN-1520216254.

Stakem, Patrick H. *RISC Microprocessors, History and Overview,* 2013, PRRB Publishing, ISBN-1520216289.

Stakem, Patrick H. *Robots and Telerobots in Space Application*s, 2011, PRRB Publishing, ISBN-1520210361.

Stakem, Patrick H. *The Saturn Rocket and the Pegasus Missions, 1965,* 2013, PRRB Publishing, ISBN-1520209916.

Stakem, Patrick H. *Visiting the NASA Centers, and Locations of Historic Rockets & Spacecraft,* 2017, PRRB Publishing, ISBN-1549651205.

Stakem, Patrick H. *Microprocessors in Space*, 2011, PRRB Publishing, ISBN-1520216343.

Stakem, Patrick H. Computer *Virtualization and the Cloud*, 2013, PRRB Publishing, ISBN-152021636X.

Stakem, Patrick H. *What's the Worst That Could Happen? Bad Assumptions, Ignorance, Failures and Screw-ups in Engineering Projects, 2014,* PRRB Publishing, ISBN-1520207166.

Stakem, Patrick H. *Computer Architecture & Programming of the Intel x86 Family, 2013,* PRRB Publishing, ISBN-1520263724.

Stakem, Patrick H. *The Hardware and Software Architecture of the Transputer,* 2011,PRRB Publishing, ISBN-152020681X.

Stakem, Patrick H. *Mainframes, Computing on Big Iron*, 2015, PRRB Publishing, ISBN- 1520216459.

Stakem, Patrick H. *Spacecraft Control Centers*, 2015, PRRB Publishing, ISBN-1520200617.

Stakem, Patrick H. *Embedded in Space,* 2015, PRRB Publishing, ISBN-1520215916.

Stakem, Patrick H. *A Practitioner's Guide to RISC Microprocessor Architecture*, Wiley-Interscience, 1996, ISBN-0471130184.

Stakem, Patrick H. *Cubesat Engineering*, PRRB Publishing, 2017, ISBN-1520754019.

Stakem, Patrick H. *Cubesat Operations*, PRRB Publishing, 2017, ISBN-152076717X.

Stakem, Patrick H. *Interplanetary Cubesats*, PRRB Publishing, 2017, ISBN-1520766173 .

Stakem, Patrick H. Cubesat Constellations, Clusters, and Swarms, Stakem, PRRB Publishing, 2017, ISBN-1520767544.

Stakem, Patrick H. *Graphics Processing Units, an overview*, 2017, PRRB Publishing, ISBN-1520879695.

Stakem, Patrick H. *Intel Embedded and the Arduino-101, 2017,* PRRB Publishing, ISBN-1520879296.

Stakem, Patrick H. *Orbital Debris, the problem and the mitigation*, 2018, PRRB Publishing, ISBN-*1980466483.*

Stakem, Patrick H. *Manufacturing in Space*, 2018, PRRB Publishing, ISBN-1977076041.

Stakem, Patrick H. *NASA's Ships and Planes*, 2018, PRRB Publishing, ISBN-1977076823.

Stakem, Patrick H. *Space Tourism*, 2018, PRRB Publishing, ISBN-

1977073506.

Stakem, Patrick H. *STEM – Data Storage and Communications*, 2018, PRRB Publishing, ISBN-1977073115.

Stakem, Patrick H. *In-Space Robotic Repair and Servicing*, 2018, PRRB Publishing, ISBN-1980478236.

Stakem, Patrick H. *Introducing Weather in the pre-K to 12 Curricula, A Resource Guide for Educators*, 2017, PRRB Publishing, ISBN-1980638241.

Stakem, Patrick H. *Introducing Astronomy in the pre-K to 12 Curricula, A Resource Guide for Educators*, 2017, PRRB Publishing, ISBN-198104065X.
Also available in a Brazilian Portuguese edition, ISBN-1983106127.

Stakem, Patrick H. *Deep Space Gateways, the Moon and Beyond*, 2017, PRRB Publishing, ISBN-1973465701.

Stakem, Patrick H. *Exploration of the Gas Giants, Space Missions to Jupiter, Saturn, Uranus, and Neptune*, PRRB Publishing, 2018, ISBN-9781717814500.

Stakem, Patrick H. *Crewed Spacecraft*, 2017, PRRB Publishing, ISBN-1549992406.

Stakem, Patrick H. *Rocketplanes to Space*, 2017, PRRB Publishing, ISBN-1549992589.

Stakem, Patrick H. *Crewed Space Stations,* 2017, PRRB Publishing, ISBN-1549992228.

Stakem, Patrick H. *Enviro-bots for STEM: Using Robotics in the pre-K to 12 Curricula, A Resource Guide for Educators,* 2017, PRRB Publishing, ISBN-1549656619.

94

Stakem, Patrick H. *STEM-Sat, Using Cubesats in the pre-K to 12 Curricula, A Resource Guide for Educators*, 2017, ISBN-1549656376.

Stakem, Patrick H. *Lunar Orbital Platform-Gateway*, 2018, PRRB Publishing, ISBN-1980498628.

Stakem, Patrick H. *Embedded GPU's*, 2018, PRRB Publishing, ISBN- 1980476497.

Stakem, Patrick H. *Mobile Cloud Robotics*, 2018, PRRB Publishing, ISBN- 1980488088.

Stakem, Patrick H. *Extreme Environment Embedded Systems,* 2017, PRRB Publishing, ISBN-1520215967.

Stakem, Patrick H. *What's the Worst, Volume-2*, 2018, ISBN-1981005579.

Stakem, Patrick H., *Spaceports*, 2018, ISBN-1981022287.

Stakem, Patrick H., *Space Launch Vehicles*, 2018, ISBN-1983071773.

Stakem, Patrick H. *Mars*, 2018, ISBN-1983116902.

Stakem, Patrick H. *X-86, 40th Anniversary ed*, 2018, ISBN-1983189405.

Stakem, Patrick H. *Lunar Orbital Platform-Gateway*, 2018, PRRB Publishing, ISBN-1980498628.

Stakem, Patrick H. *Space Weather*, 2018, ISBN-1723904023.

Stakem, Patrick H. *STEM-Engineering Process*, 2017, ISBN-1983196517.

Stakem, Patrick H. *Space Telescopes,* 2018, PRRB Publishing, ISBN-1728728568.

Stakem, Patrick H. *Exoplanets*, 2018, PRRB Publishing, ISBN-9781731385055.

Stakem, Patrick H. *Planetary Defense*, 2018, PRRB Publishing, ISBN-9781731001207.

Patrick H. Stakem *Exploration of the Asteroid Belt*, 2018, PRRB Publishing, ISBN-1731049846.

Patrick H. Stakem *Terraforming*, 2018, PRRB Publishing, ISBN-1790308100.

Patrick H. Stakem, *Martian Railroad,* 2019, PRRB Publishing, ISBN-1794488243.

Patrick H. Stakem, *Exoplanets,* 2019, PRRB Publishing, ISBN-1731385056.

Patrick H. Stakem, *Exploiting the Moon,* 2019, PRRB Publishing, ISBN-1091057850.

Patrick H. Stakem, *RISC-V, an Open Source Solution for Space Flight Computers,* 2019, PRRB Publishing, ISBN-1796434388.

Patrick H. Stakem, *Arm in Space*, 2019, PRRB Publishing, ISBN-9781099789137.

Patrick H. Stakem, *Extraterrestrial Life*, 2019, PRRB Publishing, ISBN-978-1072072188.

Stakem, Patrick H. Submarine Launched Ballistic Missiles, 2019, ISBN-978-1088954904.

Patrick H. Stakem, *Space Command*, 2019, PRRB Publishing, ISBN-978-1693005398.

www.ingramcontent.com/pod-product-compliance
Lightning Source LLC
LaVergne TN
LVHW092343060326
832902LV00008B/772